MOTHER OF $183 MILLION WINNER

MOTHER OF $183 MILLION WINNER

Catherine Gietka

To order additional copies of this book, contact:
Xlibris Corporation
1-888-795-4274
www.Xlibris.com
Orders@Xlibris.com
24748

CONTENTS

FORWARD AND DEDICATION
BY BERNADETTE GIETKA

Y es, I won $183 MILLION Dollars. Life has changed. I clean a bigger house. There are now meetings about things I never knew or cared about before. They fill my days.

My nights are all about paperwork. It magically appears in tubs at the post office, hundreds or thousands per week. My mother wrote this book. She went through a lot before the win. Of course, to me, she is the most special person in the world. We are close. She is wonderful, religious (always praying) and so willing to share this ride that I've been on. It's been more difficult than people would imagine, very complicated. But filled with a variety of experiences that are so interesting and unusual. We've had fun. My family helps with everything.

FORWARD AND DEDICATION
BY JERRY GIETKA

One hundred and eighty three MILLION Dollars. In July of 2003, my sister won the mega millions lottery. And the lives of our family will never be the same.

Sis is probably the youngest lottery winner ever, in spirit that is. She still called our parents Mommy and Daddy. Because of that, it is my guess, that she will probably be the most generous lottery winner in history as well. Of course, there are no public records to use to verify or dispute that statement. But Sis has a very strong religious philosophy and believes that she won the money for a reason. Her philanthropy will be measured in the millions of dollars and thousands of people who will be helped. She and Mom recently made some donations to several groups who provide Thanksgiving dinner to the homeless. Those contributions will feed thousands of people. Charity is a wonderful character trait, but I have recently discovered it is generally accompanied by another all too human trait. No matter how much she does, the expectations are considerably higher. Most requests are coming in with expectations of being funded for millions of dollars. When she replies with a donation of thousands or even tens of thousands, you can almost feel the disappointment in the voices of gratitude. The family has been swamped with requests.

For that reason, we have set up Mary's Fund as a foundation to support and promote the religious activities that Sis believes in. Any requests are funneled through the foundation instead of being considered individually. There is a formal review and award process with several criteria and a standing board. The two primary criteria: the request must be in support of religious activity and the request must be in writing and under $10,000. If it does not meet these criteria, a request will not be considered. My mother strongly believes that she will be able to help many more people by spreading the money around more.

Mom is 79 years old now. She raised three children as a single mom running her own business. Bernie's story became interesting because of the random selection of six numbered balls. There will be much more to come before Sis' story is completely written. But Mom's story is interesting because of the circumstances of her life. Mom is the third of six children and this book is a collection of her memories. It is being written and published as a tribute to her. It is truly amazing how vivid her memory of details is, especially nearing 80 years of age. Except for leaving out a few names and personal details, this story is typed exactly as she hand wrote it. The story is in her words and as such has very special meaning to her. And because of that, her children, Bernadette, Lynda and I, dedicate our time and resources to having her story told as she wrote it.

MOM'S BOOK

This is what my mother told me about her life in Poland.

As soon as her mother was of age to work, she got a job in another city near the Russian border. It was with a wealthy family as a maid. They had a son a few years older than her. He was away at school. When he came home for the summer he met my grandmother and fell in love with her. Within a few years, they got married. He was a cousin to the last czar, Nicholas II. He was a guard at the palace. They had two children, my mother Mary and her sister who was two years older than my mother.

Every year they had a royal ball at the palace. My grandmother could not attend. Only blood relatives were invited. My grandfather was all dressed in his uniform and he sat at the table holding my mother on his lap. The two of them were arguing about my grandmother not being able to go with him. She went into the other room to get something and when she came back, he didn't answer her. She came closer and saw that he had died holding my mother on his lap. He was 32 years old. He had a heart attack.

My mother and her sister were left with enough money to live comfortably but it was in the bank until they would be 18 years of age. My grandmother also had enough to buy a farm near her relatives. So they moved back to Makow Mazoiwiecki. After a year or two, she got married to a man with a bad temper. When he didn't like what my mother did, he beat her with a branch from a tree. Her grandmother would run to her aid and stop him.

They didn't go to school for long. Third grade was as far as my mother went. When she started school, they burned all of the Polish books and made them learn Russian. Before my mother went to school, she had to go out in the field and take care of the cows. After school, there were other chores. When they went to the market place, there were a lot of Jewish people who owned the stalls. My mother talked to them and learned how to speak Jewish. She also learned French when she was living in her father's house. She had a nanny from France who took care of her before her father died.

The winters in Poland get pretty bad. The snow was so deep, it is a wonder they got to school and back home without getting lost in the snow.

My aunt, my mother's sister, was sent to America at 16 years of age. She got married and my mother was sent to America at age 14. They thought life was easier here and they would have a better life here. My mother's boat was the last one to get through. The next one was sent back since the first World war started. Her boat hit an iceberg but it didn't sink. They repaired it and made it to New York safely.

When she got off the boat in New York, it was the first time she saw a black person. She thought that people worked so much, they didn't have time to take a bath.

She went to live with her sister until her sister's first two children were born. It got too crowded so she went to live with friends of her family. They had a daughter who was her age and those two became as close as sisters. This was in Baltimore, MD. Jobs were scarce so they went to New York to work in tailor shops. My father met my mother in Baltimore before she went to New York. He went to see her every week on the weekends. He proposed to her and she got engaged and came back to Baltimore to get married.

Her life changed into a nightmare. She had 6 children and had to work to support them. My father was an alcoholic. He worked but he spent all of his money in the bar. The first apartment they rented was too small, so they moved to another. This one had water. In the other one they had to carry buckets of water. They got the water at the marketplace which was 3 blocks away. This place had water but no electric. The lights were gas lights. No radio. We had to go to my aunt's house—two miles away—to listen to the radio on weekends, or to a friend's house who had electricity in their house. It sure was a drastic change in my mother's life. From being born with a silver spoon in her mouth to this. The money in the bank that her father left her was bombed in the war.

I don't remember the first apartment. I was about two years old when we left. The new one was next door to a bakery. That saved us from being hungry. As soon as we were old enough, one of us got a job in the bakery. I was about 8 years old when I started to baby-sit. We didn't get paid with money. We got a loaf of bread and some buns that didn't sell that day. That was during the depression. Most people had to eat bread and lard. We had butter on our bread. The owner of the bakery would cook a big pot of soup and she gave me a bowl while I worked there. I was in my glory. I felt like I was a rich little girl. They had a room on the second floor with a player piano. When they had company downstairs, I had to take their three year old girl upstairs and play and sing with her. That wasn't work, that was fun.

I didn't have it so bad. My sister and brother did the most work. My brother was six years older than I was. He went to work in the bakery. My oldest sister had to take care of the other four children while my mother went to work in the cannery. My brother Steve was a baby and my brother Tony was two going on three. I was five and my sister Betty was seven. The eldest girl, Ida, was nine and the oldest boy, Walter, was 11. Ida would sit in a rocker at night, with the two youngest boys on her lap. I would sit on one arm of the rocker and Betty on the other arm. We would sing for hours. That rocker really got used.

In the summer, my mother took us to a farm. Where people went to pick beans and make a few dollars for school tuition and books. We were Catholic and didn't want to go to public school which was free, so we helped to earn a little. My mother didn't make us work much. When the sun came out and it got hot, she told us to find a shady spot under a tree and stay cool. We thought we had the best mother because the other children had to work all day.

One summer my brother did something to get a farmer mad. That farmer told my mother that, as punishment, he would have to pick a field of tomatoes. That would take a week or more. But he was smart. He got all of the children there to go with him the next morning and they got it done in one day. He didn't have to pick any at all. He did things like that. He wanted a new pair of shoes. There wasn't enough money to buy them. The next day he put his old shoes in the oven until they were very well done. He did get his shoes but only after a well deserved spanking.

My sister, Betty, wanted to cook a pot of soup while my mother was working. We could pick beans but we weren't old enough to work in the cannery. She went to a field and took a load of cabbage and almost got shot by the farmer. It was probably a warning shot, but it sure scared us. They let us take some of the beans and tomatoes from the cannery. She made her soup but got punished for taking the cabbage.

When Betty was about 9 years old, I was seven. Together with about six other children from the neighborhood, we decided to go into the junk business. All morning we went to the big stores and collected boxes and paper. We folded them flat and tied them into a neat bundle. We had a wagon to haul them down to the junkyard about 12 blocks away. It was a hot summer day and we were thirsty. On the way we passed a soda factory.

The men working there felt sorry for us. They only had one bottle of soda. They gave it to us and we shared it. We didn't get to drink a soda very often, so it tasted great. We got the wagon to the junkyard and earned 2cents ($.02). Now, the problem was, how to divide it. There was a candy store nearby. The owner didn't have much patience with us. It only took us about half an hour to choose the most candy we could get. It was a big decision. The licorice candy hats were 15 for a penny. We got 30 of those. Each one of us got four except that there were two short. The youngest ones got shorted and I was one of those. We tried to make the candy last as long as we could. Instead of chewing the candy, we let it melt in our mouth slowly. I had mine for hours. Just so you will know how much 2 cents was worth in those days, I will tell you.

My mother worked about 14 hours in the cannery each day and she made about 50 cents. Our apartment rent was $9.00 a month. Most of the time there was not enough money. Our landlady liked me so I was the one chosen to go to her house and tell her we couldn't pay the whole month's rent but my mother would make it up the next month. That landlady lived about eight blocks from us. That was the longest walk I had to make. I kept on rehearsing the speech I had to tell her. By the time I got to her house, I was shaking like a leaf on a windy day. She was so nice, instead of giving me a sermon to take back to my mother, she gave me a lollypop. The way back home was much sweeter than the way going to her house.

One year before Christmas, I had a nickel. I think I found it because I never earned that much. Every day, I would go window shopping with my sisters. You had to be careful how to spend all that money. We went to Broadway and looked in every store on that street thinking about buying this or that. The next day we went to Highlandtown. And then the third day we went uptown. Those stores were too expensive but we were hoping to get some things on sale. After all, we had six children and two adults. That was eight presents to buy for 5 cents. I did my homework pretty well. I chose a card with a few barrettes on it for two cents. That took care of two of my sisters and my mother. A bag of combs came in handy. That was enough for my three brothers and my father and cost two cents as well. I kept the penny that was left over for a long time before I spent it. It made me feel that we weren't penniless after all. If it were not for the war, the bank that my mother's fortune was in would not have been bombed and we would have been wealthy.

The best time of the year was Christmas eve. We celebrated it with the whole family getting together. My two aunts, their husbands, eleven cousins and all eight of us. That was 23 people all together in one kitchen. We called the holiday "Wigilja". You had to fast all day and no meat was allowed that day. Only seafood was served.

The kitchen was too small for all of the children getting in the way while all of the ladies were cooking. My mother told us to go outside and sit on the front steps. We were told to look up at the sky and look for the star to appear (the one that the three Kings and the shepherds followed to the manger where Jesus was born). We sat there about an hour. Finally the star shone up in the sky. We went running into the house shouting "Jesus is born". We really believed it was the star. Wasn't it? Those are some of the memories I didn't mind remembering.

Mother's day was both a happy and sad time for my brother Walter one year. He worked at the bakery and at the movie theater to earn a few pennies. He saved up for a long time to buy a big potted snowball flower for my mother. When everyone went to sleep, he put it out in the alley and closed the gate so no one would steal it. In the morning he ran out to bring it into the house. It was in pieces. My father came home late and drunk and knocked it over and broke it. I think my brother was angry with my father for a long while.

My sister Ida was told by my mother not to let any boy touch her knee. If he did that or kissed her, she would be pregnant. When she went out with a boy the first time, he kissed her good night. He was so puzzled because she started crying and ran into the house. My mother asked her what was wrong and she said she was pregnant. After 20 questions, she finally stopped crying and found out the truth. Years later I found out that most mothers told that story to their daughters.

Our greatest problem was learning how to speak to the children in the neighborhood. My mother only spoke Polish and so we all spoke Polish in the house. I didn't learn English until I went to school. At first, I felt embarrassed. The other children made fun of me. My day came when I could get back at them. They couldn't speak Polish. We had a half day learning Polish in school and the other half in English. I could speak two languages and they could speak only one. Another thing was that I was left handed. The nun at school would hit my left hand with a ruler and tell me to write with my right hand. Soon I could write with both. When I played ball or jump rope I used my left hand more than my right hand.

I was a good student but could never be first on the honor role. I was always 3rd or 4th. Every month the girl and boy that were

1st or 2nd stayed that way for the entire eight years of grade school. I was 3rd one month and a boy was 4th. We went back and forth that way until we graduated. I was in all the plays they had at school because we got out of a lot of class work when we had to rehearse. I didn't work when I joined the choir. Rehearsals were after school. We had a beautiful music teacher, a nun named Sister Isabel. She had a voice like a movie star. She was about 90 years old but looked about 60.

When I was about six years old, my mother had her last baby. He died at birth. It was a choice of him or my mother. The Doctor saved my mother. That baby weighed about 15 pounds.

A few years later, my brother Walter woke up in the middle of the night and said that someone had spilled cold water on his legs. The next morning a telegram came to let my mother know that her mother had died in Poland. She was about 53 years old. My mother still had three half sisters and two half brothers who were born after she had left Poland.

The most heavenly time of my life was when I received my first Holy Communion. I was 10 years old. I thought that nothing could stop me from going to heaven when I die. In my mind, only Catholics would go to heaven. I was so glad I was born a Catholic. I thought that I had it made. Little did I know I had to spend the rest of my life fighting the devil who is always trying to get you to commit sins so he can have your soul and take it to hell. I hope that I have won over him so far and will for the rest of my life. On one of my trips to Europe, a nun told our group that anyone could become a "saint". Even if they were the worst sinner, as long as you repent and change your life and try to make up for what you did in the past. Good, there is hope for me yet.

My aunt was having some problems in her marriage. She asked my mother to move into her house and we did. It is hard to change schools. Our school was about a mile away. Since we didn't want to change we walked that far every day. There was a school about one block away and another four blocks further. But we walked the one mile. We only had to do it for two years.

My brother Tony was about nine years old and my cousin, my aunt's daughter, was about seven. He had heard about the circus parade and knew how to get there to it. It was about six blocks from the house. So the two of them went to see it. They sat on the curb for about an hour and finally saw the parade start. When the elephants came by, he told our cousin to look at what the elephants were doing. She said: "you brought me here and we waited all this time for that?" Her mother and my mother were ready to call the police, thinking something had happened to them. They both got a spanking and were punished. They didn't have to be grounded. She never went with him anywhere again. My aunt sold the house and we were on the move again.

This time it wasn't an apartment. My mother found a house for sale. It was $900. Someone didn't pay the mortgage that was due and the Building and Loan Company was selling it to get their money back. Big problem. You needed $100 to get the loan. My mother asked her older sister to lend her the money. She would not because my father was a bad risk. Of course, he didn't bring any money home.

My mother came home and was crying. My brother Walter asked her why she was crying. When she told him the whole story, he went into the other room and came back with a big jar full of change. He counted out $100 and gave it to her. He had saved the money he had earned instead of spending it on himself. He was 16 years old and so mature for his age. He took it upon himself to help support the family. He took my father's place. That was the first house we called our own. The good part was, the school was only six blocks from that house, especially in the winter. I still had two more years until graduation.

Since my brother worked in the theater, he got passes to see the movies. All you had to pay was a few cents for tax. My sisters and I got to see a lot of pictures. Those were the days of the big Hollywood stars. It wasn't just one movie house he worked in. There were a few others. He became assistant manager.

My aunt was working so my cousins spent a lot of time at our house. After school my cousin and I played games until my mother came home from work. I would walk my cousin home. We lived one block from a park. We walked through the park, a short cut, saved a lot of time. Her brothers came at night to play cards on the weekends. We were a close family.

After I graduated, I took a job in the same bakery, as a sales girl this time. I was fifteen and had to get a permit. After sixteen you didn't need one. My brother Walter was in the army. The second world war had begun. My sister Betty worked in a defense factory as a sweater. My oldest sister worked in a car dealership in the office.

A few months later my father had a heart attack. He passed away a few days later. Walter was in California. He just made it home as we were going to the cemetery. He had to go back right after. My mother still went to the farm for the summer. I had to quit my job and go with her and my two younger brothers. When we got back to the city, I went to work in a cookie factory, making the boxes for the cookies.

My friends and I were in the movies watching the news. The boys were joking about going into the army soon. One of them did go into the army. As soon as his training was over he went overseas and was killed as soon as they reached the beach.

I had to quit my job again. Back to the farm for the summer. It wasn't so bad this time. I met the boss' son. He worked in the field with us. When we filled a bag of beans he would weigh the bags. He asked me to go to the movies. His father had to ask our boss who was in charge of the people who came to work there from the city. She was a friend of my mother's.

One day my mother got a letter from Walter. He had to have an operation. It was a small thing but she felt bad. The big boss, my boyfriend's father, saw her crying. He found out about the letter (it was her birthday), he went to the corner store and bought a cake and brought it to her while she was working to make her feel better. He would have been a good father-in-law. I broke up with his son two years later.

When we came home, I went to work at Bethlehem Steel. You had to be eighteen to get a job there. Most of the men were getting drafted and they lowered the age limit to seventeen. The war changed a lot of things. Food was rationed and so was gas. You had to get coupons for both. Everyone tried to do what they could to help end the war. Even the movie stars worked hard selling war bonds and entertaining the boys here and overseas. They worked in the canteens serving food and dancing with them. I went to one of the camps with my sister and her girlfriend. A bus would come into the city and pick up the girls. After the dance, the bus would take them back.

My brother Walter came home safe after the war was over.

I worked in the mill. They were having a banquet that year and were putting together a show. We were hula dancers in Hawaii. We had to go to rehearsals in the big boss' house. One night a big storm started before we left for home. The boss was a lady. She was mean at work but really nice after work. She asked me to stay at her house that night and go to work with her and her husband in the morning. I had to call my mother and ask her permission. At first she said no, but after talking with my boss, she agreed to let me stay. It was getting worse outside with raining and thunder and lightning. I was glad to stay.

When it was time to go to sleep, she (the boss) knelt down and prayed with me. I didn't expect that because she wasn't Catholic. She was a religious person, I found out. When we woke up, coffee was ready. Her husband woke up earlier and fixed breakfast. He also had two lunch bags ready for us to take to work.

The big celebration was held in the Lord Baltimore hotel. We put on a good show. That night I met Ben (my husband). With the gas shortage, the people who had a car, took as many riders as they could. He asked me if I wanted to be one of his riders. I was glad to get a ride. The street cars were crowded in the morning and you had to stand up for about an hour going to work. It felt awful when you were still half asleep and wished you had a seat. After a few months I went out with him. It got to the point of no return. I guess I was meant for him and he was meant for me.

My mother wasn't happy about my dating him. He was divorced and she knew we couldn't get married in church. He was only nineteen when he got married the first time. You couldn't get an annulment in church back then. We got married by a justice of the peace. I always felt guilty and felt bad when I couldn't go to confession and receive Holy Communion. We lived in an apartment in the country. He had pigeons and was busy with them and had meetings at night. I didn't like being out there at night. He wouldn't move back into the city. We disagreed so much and I was expecting our first child. One day I got really angry at him and when my mother asked if I wanted to come home, I packed fast. I got my way. He moved back into the city.

We lived with my mother for two years. My brother always wanted his own business. A house with a store front was on sale. My mother sold the house we lived in and bought it for him. We moved again. I went to work for a few months and quit to have our second child. It got too crowded living with my mother because my oldest sister got married and lived there also. A house was on sale two doors away. It was a fixer upper, a real rat trap. We fixed it ourselves and made it livable. It was a three apartment house. We could live in one apartment, my oldest sister in the other and then his brother in the third. We only needed $200 to buy it. We got a loan for $3300. The rent would pay for the mortgage.

Ben sold his car for the $200 and we had our first house. It was ready to move in when I came home from the hospital with Bernadette. Jerry (the first born) was two years old. Ben had to get a ride to work until he got another used car. He knew a lot about cars and could fix some parts himself. He liked to take an old car and get it to run again. I never had to worry about finances. When we needed a few dollars, he managed to get into some business. Selling pigeons was his first love. Then he tried jewelry, women's clothes from the 20's, men's shoes and many others I didn't know of. He even started a medical supply business. His cousin was his partner. They didn't make a fortune but they made a lot of poor people happy. If someone couldn't pay for a bed or other things, they let them have it for free. He still kept his job as a foreman at Bethlehem Steel. I only gave him $5 a week for gas and lunch. He had enough, making extra money. His cousin had a restaurant in the factory. A lot of meals were free.

That's how he managed to buy pigeons and feed them. He was seven years old when his father let him take care of his pigeons. We had thousands later until he was 88 years old.

The house was so much fun to live in. When I put the children to bed, my sister and sister-in-law came down to the first floor and we played cards, sometimes forgetting how late it was. One night we were laughing too loud and woke Ben up. We had been drinking some peach brandy. A Jewish neighbor made it herself and gave me a bottle. We felt no pain and didn't get tired. We looked at the time and it was about 5 am in the morning. We sure played the night away. They went up to their apartments.

When Ben's mother came to dinner a few weeks later, he brought out the peach brandy and bragged how good it tasted. I tried to tell them that it didn't turn out so good this time. I had filled the bottle with some water. We didn't want the men to know how much we did drink that night. It must not have tasted too bad since they liked it.

One night we were sitting on the front steps. I put Bernie to sleep and Jerry was playing around the light pole. He started climbing it and I was afraid that he would get hurt, so I told him to stop. He kept it up. I took him from the pole into the house. As soon as I got to the door, I heard a loud noise. I turned and saw a street car coming toward the house. My sister was still sitting in the chair. She was shocked and couldn't move. Her friend that was with us jumped up and ran up the street but didn't have time to help my sister. I was afraid to look, but, thank God, the street car stopped about a foot from her chair. The worst scene was the pole Jerry was climbing. A car was wrapped around it. If he wasn't disobedient, he might have been crushed. I do believe in miracles.

The same accident happened to me when I was seven. My sister Betty was nine. We played a game trying to jump across the alley in two jumps. One of the children was supposed to watch that no car or truck was driving past. It was Betty's turn to keep an eye out for me. I had to run about a half block and take a big leap. She didn't do a good job looking for the car or truck. As I leaped, I didn't make it across the alley. As I lay under the huge truck, against a giant wheel, I heard: "there is a truck coming." Too late. I was more embarrassed than hurt. I was standing up before the police came, watching water run down the pavement, hoping they didn't see it. I was busy begging them not to tell my mother. I said I was all right. They had to take me home and fill out their report. I was scared of getting a spanking for playing the game. My mother was glad the wheel didn't run over me. I would have been crushed. Miracle?

Not long after that my father had some long boards with nails in them out in the yard. He was taking the nails out and cutting the boards into small pieces for the winter. They were used for starting a fire in the coal stove to heat the house. I was walking across the boards and tripped and fell on one of the nails. It went into the palm of my hand and came out the other side. My father pulled my hand up and my mother poured peroxide over it so I wouldn't get an infection. She also wrapped it tightly to stop the bleeding. The doctor said that she did a good job. It didn't affect the use of my hand. I'd say God had a hand in that too. I started to think I was a tomboy or a klutz.

The next year I learned how to crochet. After Bernadette was born, I wanted a bed spread. It was for my mother for Mother's day. I worked on it every chance I could, when the babies took their nap and after they went to sleep at night. Eight hours every day for a full year, and I finished it a day before Mother's day. I had to pick the hardest pattern there was. It was only used for holidays, so it is still in good shape after 58 years. Ben's sister was good at paper hanging. She taught me how to do it and I did a pretty good job. Saved a lot of money doing your own work. I was a good painter too. I even laid tiles on the floor, the hallway and the steps. When you live in a three story house, that's a lot of steps. I was a fast learner. Even put up congo wall in the kitchen and I saved $500 on that job. I was only fair as a cook. I did cook a delicious pot of shrimp soup. Nobody could cook it as good as I could. My round steak was great.

We couldn't afford a refrigerator or a washing machine and for a year I had to wash clothes by hand on a wash board. In my spare time I had to help in the store. I washed and ironed clothes for my older sister and for my mother. They both worked. The few dollars they gave me, I saved for a refrigerator and a washing machine. No more hand washing. It took me at least eight hours a day to iron. The clothes weren't wash and wear then. You had to starch the boy's shirts. The full apron my mother wore in the store had to be starched. When I bought wash and wear clothes later you can be sure I didn't do any ironing any more. Even if they had to be ironed, I sent them to Poland to my cousins.

My sister Betty was getting married. My brother had a new kitchen installed and she couldn't get dressed there, so she came to our house and we got dressed together. I was her maid of honor and Ben was one of the ushers. I had the best children. They behaved very nice for my mother and my oldest sister who took them to the church. Jerry was four years old and Bernadette was two years old. Finally my oldest sister's mother-in-law had an apartment empty and they went to live with her. About a year later, Ben's brother and his wife found a house and they moved. So my other sister Betty and her husband took the apartment on the third floor. They had a son a year later.

I was expecting my third baby. Lynda was not born beautiful but each day she got more beautiful. Jerry was handsome the first day. There were 27 babies born in that hospital then. All girls except for one boy. He had brown eyes and the nurses were all bragging about him. They said that the girl babies were all flirting with him. It was labor day when Bernadette was born. The first thing the Doctor said when he came in was: "you take Labor day seriously." But I really didn't. No labor pains or even a stomach ache. I could have had her when I went shopping and brought her home in a shopping bag. She was an angel even then. She looked just like Jerry but as they grew he looked just like his father Ben and she looked just like me.

I loved them all, even when I felt like getting angry when they were bad. I couldn't stay angry with them for long. They were irresistible. The best kids in the world, and they were and are mine. Thanks be to God. Without God, I don't know if I could have gone through some bad times so easily. Everything that ever happened turned out well in the end.

They say your life changes every seven years. Seemed like mine changed every three years. Now it was Betty coming downstairs to play cards. The only sad part about my sister-in-law moving was her daughter missed playing with our children. She loved changing the babies' diapers and going shopping on Broadway. She mentioned that many years later. Another baby for my sister Betty. She wanted a girl this time. Right before the baby was born, my brother Walter had trouble with his health. He went to the Doctor and the result came back. He had a bad spleen. If they operated, he could die because it spread into his blood and they couldn't be sure he could survive. He was happy about the baby. He hoped to be well enough to see the baby. The Doctor told him he had about six months. He didn't want to tell my mother but she went to the Doctor and found out for herself. She was not the same after that. Took the news very hard. That's why he didn't want to tell her.

The baby was born and it was a girl. When Betty came home with the baby, I knew something was wrong. Her eyes were different than any other baby. She turned all around in the crib. Betty and her husband thought they had a strong baby. When she was four days old they had a feeling that something was wrong. They called a Doctor that night and were told they were over protective parents. The next morning that baby died. The reason she had been turning around was because she must have been in pain. The Doctor told us that it was a blessing because the baby had been born without a rectum. As she grew older, they would have had to operate many times. She would have suffered all of her life.

Betty took it so hard she couldn't go up to her own apartment. I let her stay downstairs. But after a few weeks, Ben said if she didn't go back upstairs, she would never get over it. Her husband and her son needed her. It worked. She went upstairs and was well enough to take care of them. Since I was supposed to be the baby's Godmother, I bought the stone for her grave, a beautiful angel. I didn't have much money but the angel was in the window and was on sale, from $300 down to $150. I was lucky. Just had to iron clothes a little longer, I didn't mind.

Walter was getting weaker as the months went by. Soon he couldn't work in the store and had to spend more time in the hospital. When he came home for the weekend, he had to spend a lot of time in bed. I helped my mother in the store as much as I could. Lynda was two years old and loved to dance. She wanted to cheer Walter up. He liked watching her, until one day she picked her foot up and twisted around too close to his bed and kicked him in the leg. The one that had the sore on it. She didn't dance so close to him after that.

I had a little time one week and straightened out the shelves and shined the soda fountain. I worked hard but it was worth it to see the look on his face when he walked in and said: "what did you do? It looks like a new store." He loved his store. Even Ben didn't complain about me spending more time in the store. He was busy with his pigeons. Those six months stretched into a year and a half. The spleen grew so big, he joked about being pregnant. He couldn't take it any more and decided to get operated on. He survived the operation but developed Leukemia. It got worse every day. His skin got a yellow color and the whites of his eyes were yellow. We went to the hospital the last day and the nurse said he must be waiting for someone. He was waiting for the rest of us to come in and his eyes turned the most beautiful blue.

They say that if you pray to the Blessed Mother, she is with you when your time is near. He looked so happy, she must have been with him. He was 33 years old when he died. Since he was in the army he had a military funeral with a 21 gun salute at the cemetery. My mother cried every day for years.

My brother Tony was in the Navy and was stationed in Norfolk. Ida and her husband took a week off from work and took our mother to visit Tony. It still didn't stop her from crying every day when she got back home. My mother decided to sell the store.

Ida didn't want it. None of the others were interested in it. I wasn't getting along with Ben and thought that if I was left with the children, I wouldn't have to leave home if I took the store because the store was a part of the house. I decided to take a chance and see if I could do it. We bought the store. My mother bought a house and Tony was supposed to live with her after the navy. Betty also bought a house next door to our mother. Ida bought a house and our youngest brother Steve moved with her. He just got out of the army. He went to college, graduated and got married. He bought a house too.

I got a divorce from Ben. It was hard on the children. We used to spend every Sunday visiting his sister. They had a house on the waterfront. In the winter we went to my mother's house for dinner. In the summer, it was to his sister's house at the shore. The children still went with Ben for a while but he met someone and got remarried. It only lasted three years. He still tried to come back to me but I was still angry with him. I thought I would never talk to him again.

When Tony came home from the navy, he bought another house and my mother did not have a car. She couldn't drive anyway. She moved back into town with me and helped to take care of the children. I bought a house near my brother Steve. I loved it but I didn't realize how nerve wracking it would be to get back and forth to the city. The traffic was awful. We decided to use it in the summer. And stay in the city in the winter. It was hard to drive when it snowed. I couldn't decide where to live so I put the store up for sale, as well as the new house. Whichever one would sell first, then that was where we would live. The newer house sold as soon as I called the real estate agent. We moved back into the store.

Bernadette had gone to school to be a nun. After four years, she decided not to stay and came home. Lynda got married for two months and then she came home. They were arguing and she was expecting. She was smart and she left him right away. History repeating itself. Jerry got married. When he went to get a job he found out he could get a better one with a college degree. He had dropped out before and now he went back and finished his four year degree and got a much better job. He kept on getting better jobs as the years went by, finally retiring from State government. He loved being on stage and played in college plays and in some dinner theatres and others. He dreamed of having his own theatre one day. Time will tell.

After I sold the house, Bernadette came home from school and wanted to live there. Too late. Jerry wanted it too after

he got married. But, too late, I already
sold it. Lynda and my mother were glad
to get back to the city. Just before I sold
the summer house, the riots broke out
in the city. We went to stay in that house
for a few days until they were over. I was
anxious to see if the store was even still
there. Some of the stores near there were
burnt down. Luckily ours was all right. I
was still living a charmed life.

I did good in the store and had five
houses. All bought with the rent I collected
from three of them. I kept the store and a
little house next door. I bought that one
for $1,000. Bernadette had a dog and we
didn't have a yard for the dog. The house
would make a good doghouse. After the
dog died, I was going to demolish the
house and make a yard. A young couple
needed a house to rent and later to buy
it. They said they would give me a down

payment and pay for it as rent. The boy got into a lot of debt and moved so no one could find him. He already paid the $1,000 for the house. I started to think about the yard again. An elderly man needed to rent a place right away. I thought he would be there just a few years. It was 17 years later when he passed away and he didn't have a will. I felt sorry for him and only took $75 a month for rent. He left a half million dollars!

Since I was the closest thing to a relative, being his landlady, I was made the executor of his estate. I got $10,000 for the executor's fee. A brother and sister were found and they got $100,000 each. The lawyers got the rest. That was the most expensive doghouse I ever bought. Things were getting better though.

Lynda got married again. A house went on sale across the street from the store.

I took them over to see the house. They wanted $10,000 for it. The agent said that if I bought it today, it would only be $7,500. I asked Lynda if she wanted an expensive wedding or a cheaper one and the house. They chose the house. Their wedding was still very nice. We had a nice hall, a caterer who didn't charge an arm and a leg. A Polish orchestra and good friends and family to attend the wedding. It was in church and her gown was fit for a princess. She looked like one walking down the long aisle of our parish church.

Ben said I always used a dollar as if it were rubber. I stretched it as far as I could. I gave Jerry a down payment on his house. He sold it 15 years later at a good profit, nearly five times what he paid for it. Now that is stretching the dollar. Bernadette got the house three doors down from Lynda. I always treated them all equally.

My mother sewed nightgowns for Jerry when he was a baby. They were still in good condition for Bernadette and Lynda to wear. The crib also went down from one to the other—equal, huh?

One day my mother went to visit a sick friend. She came back with a brochure advertising a trip to Poland and Rome. It was for three weeks and only cost $595.00 and it included the air fare, hotel, meals and tours. She was so sad. She wanted to go, but didn't want to go by herself. I said that I would go with her. I could afford to close the store for a few weeks.

The children were married. No babies to worry about. I was excited about my first trip to Europe. When the tickets came I realized that I had to go on a plane. I was standing outside and just then a plane was flying by. I looked up and said: "No way am I going to be all the way up there on a plane!" There was a holy picture with a prayer on the back of it. It said: "if you have a fear of planes just put yourself in the hands of God and leave it up to destiny." My fear left me right then and I not only made that trip but seven more to Europe and back. Then I made more than a half dozen more in the States.

It was a great trip and the group was the greatest I ever went with. There were 750 people from all over the United States. We were going for the beatification of Fr. Maximilian Kolbe. He was the priest that gave up his life in Germany so another man could live. That man had a wife and two sons. It was during WWII and before that war ended those two sons had been killed. The man's wife died and he was left alone. He spent the rest of his life traveling all over the world helping to promote

the canonization of Fr. Kolbe. I had the
privilege of attending that ceremony in
Rome in 1980. It was so crowded, all the
hotels, convents, rectories were filled.
Part of the group had to ride a half hour
outside Rome to get a room. I was with
that group and it gave us a chance to see
another town. Fr. Kolbe worked in Japan
converting a lot of Japanese to become
Catholics. There were thousands of them
in Rome.

We walked in a procession, in the
Vatican Gardens to the grotto near the
house that Pope John XXIII liked to live
in. He spent some time playing with the
children who visited. Some of the children
I knew. Jerry went with a girl in America,
she was one of ten children. Her aunt lived
across from the Vatican. They went to visit
her in the summer. The Pope's secretary
knew her father and he introduced them

to the Pope. When they were allowed to visit him they played in the gardens. Jerry did not marry her, they broke up before I could travel to Rome.

We visited the four major Basilicas: the Vatican, St. Mary Major, St. John Laterum and St. Paul outside the walls. On one trip I walked on the road that leads to St. Paul outside the wall. That's the one St. Peter took when he was leaving Rome after the death of Jesus. As he was walking, he saw Jesus going to Rome. Jesus told him that someone had to be in Rome to take care of his people. St. Peter was ashamed and went back. He was beheaded and hung upside down on the cross.

The Coliseum was full of cats. Years later Bernadette went with me on a trip to Rome and I told her to look at all the cats. Not one was there. It was a meat shortage that year. We didn't eat much meat that trip. We visited the Catacombs, the Spanish Steps, the Birthday Cake, the fountain where you throw the three coins while standing backward to get your wish. They sell the best ice cream near the fountain.

It was the year Cardinal Wyszynski was freed and he was in a small church, St. Stanislaus. When we went into the church there he was with 65 priests and bishops that were in our group. They were lined up and shook hands with everyone. We kissed the Cardinal's ring and talked to a lot of priests who were familiar with our parish. We also met an author from Poland. He had tea and cookies ready for us. He took a picture with the group. We stood on some steps and about a hundred at a time fit into the picture. I enjoyed the tours but was anxious to get back to the hotel. I had my money in a belt and when

I went to sleep I put it under my pillow. Getting dressed in a hurry, I forgot to put it on. When I finally got back to the hotel, it was there.

We went to the big hall to have an audience with the Pope. There was a Bishop next to my mother. He looked just like my brother. He told us the history of the big hall. He was from Poland and my mother enjoyed talking to him about Poland.

We went to Florence and saw the statue of David. We visited the churches and museums, then on to see the leaning tower of Pisa. One lady put her fingers to the side and said that she would hold it up while we walked inside. Then we spent the night in Assisi. We went to mass at St. Francis Basilica. Then we walked a half hour to the top of the hill to St. Claire's. Our hotel was there at the top of the mountain.

We went back to Rome and saw the
Sistine chapel. Michelangelo painted the
ceiling lying on his back on a scaffold and
he took many years to paint it. His Pieta
was in St. Peter's Basilica. Someone took
a hammer and broke a part of it. They did
repair it and put it behind iron gates. I'm
glad I saw it and got to touch it. We kissed
the foot of St. Peter's statue. So many
people kissed the foot, the toe looks like
it was wearing away.

We packed to go to Poland for the next
two weeks. We would tour Poland and
then spend a week with family. We started
from Warsaw. Our guide took us to see
the church Fr. Kolbe and his community
built. We made a pilgrimage to Our Lady
of Czestochowa (Jasna Gora), where many
miracles happened. I was happy to visit
Chopin's birthplace. I learned to play the
piano years later and played his songs

better than any other. Bernadette was my teacher.

When we went to Krakow we spent the night there. It is a beautiful city. We went down into the salt mines. It was very scary. You keep thinking of a cave-in. I soon forgot my fear. The guide taking us on that tour looked just like Robert Redford. They built a cathedral in the mines and the statues were perfect. Hitler had his parties down there so they couldn't get bombed. When we got to the water, the guide told us that people came in that way in small boats until one boat capsized and everyone drowned. It's salt water and you had to be about a foot over the water to be able to breathe.

There was a gift shop and a tea shop. The gifts were made of the salt from the mines. They told us to keep them covered or the air would make them disappear.

Our guide took his hammer and broke a piece of the salt off and gave it to me. It has been 36 years and I still have it. It was uncovered for a few years. The crosses that we bought did fall apart. The pieces are still there. Back to Warsaw.

My cousins came to the hotel and took us to their apartment in Grodzisk. Her daughter lived in Ursus. It took about a half hour to drive there. Her mother and father lived in another city and came to meet us. They could only stay one day. The next day was All Souls day. Her apartment was only a few blocks from the cemetery. We could walk there. Some elderly women sat in front of the cemetery selling flowers. The priest had a Mass first and then said the rosary. It must have been over a thousand people attending. Mothers brought their children and babies in carriages. The streets were full of people walking to the cemetery all day. We went back to the apartment, on the second floor, and looked out of the window. It was just getting dark and they put big candles on the graves and lit them. We could see the whole cemetery lit up looking like a Christmas garden. After all these years, I can still see it.

I went to Mass every morning. The church was only a few blocks away. One lady in our group didn't have a family to visit so my cousin invited her to stay with us. She went to the church with me. Walking back to the apartment, we passed a bakery. I wanted to surprise my cousin with hot fresh rolls for breakfast. I went in and ordered a dozen rolls. The lady put them on the counter and I paid her. She stood there and I stood there waiting for her to put them in a bag. Then I remembered my cousin carried a shopping bag with her. Now I knew why. They didn't give you a bag. Luckily my pocketbook was big enough to hold half a dozen. The lady with me had one too. We went out on the street with rolls peeking out of our bags. My cousin's son was on his way to school and saw us. He was laughing. It must have looked very funny. We all had a good laugh back at the apartment.

My cousin took me to Warsaw on a train. I kept sliding on the seat and almost fell to the floor of the train. The seats were very slippery. They tried to get me to drive their car but I wouldn't. They drive too fast in Poland.

My cousin's husband was a director of a bank. He had about thirty employees in his bank. When she took me there she had to rap on the door and wait for them to open the door for us. I didn't have a problem changing my money to "Zlotys". My cousin worked in a hospital, in case we needed medicine we might be able to get it easily. Before they moved to Grodzisk, they lived in Makov Mazowiecki. He was the mayor of that town. It was interesting to see all of the mementoes and gifts he had from that job.

The Communists were still in Poland at that time. With the job he had, they weren't allowed to go to church or have religious objects in the house. When their babies had to be baptized, they went to visit her mother in the other towns and baptized them there. Their salary was about $10 a month. Rent was $10 a month. One salary went for rent, the other for food. If they made any extra money and saved a little, the bank would match the money they saved for their children. That way if the children got married they would have a good start in life. Not many people could save anything.

My cousin gave me a vase about a foot tall and heavy. It was an expensive crystal vase. I didn't like carrying any heavy luggage but didn't want to be rude. So I managed to bring it home in one piece. My mother gave it to my son. I saw that same vase in New York in a shop window. It was $125.00. I have it today. My son moved a few times and it keeps coming back to me.

I forgot to tell the story of how my cousin in Poland met her husband. When she was 16 years old she was taken to the concentration camp. The general needed a maid and housekeeper for his wife. She was the one they chose. They made her sleep in the barn with the horses. One day she read the cards for the General's wife and told her to make some excuse to keep the General at home. He was supposed to go up on a plane with the other soldiers on an important mission. She convinced him to stay home. That plane was bombed and everyone on it was killed. The wife was so grateful to my cousin, she let her sleep in the house until the war was over. My cousin used to sneak some bread to the prisoners. Her future husband was one of them.

Before I left Poland she read the cards for me and saw a baby that was born dead. My daughter Lynda was expecting her 2nd baby in a few months. I was anxious until the baby was born. He was a healthy boy and is still living. A year later Lynda gave birth to a baby girl. That made five grandchildren.

My mother seemed to be forgetting things. Soon she could not go out by herself. She had a stroke. She got well enough to come home but was senile. She was like a two year old child. She was bed ridden for four years. At first, I had to feed her baby food. She couldn't swallow any food except if it was ground up in a blender.

Bernadette liked to travel. So did my mother. We bought a wheel chair and a blue Suburban. We took her everywhere we went. She loved Disney World. When we went to the park, they took us into the shows before letting anyone else in. We didn't have to wait in the long lines. Whenever we came home, she wanted to go again. I closed the store for two months in the summer and we went to Atlantic City, Wildwood, Ocean City, etc. The only time I left her home was when we went to Europe. My brother asked her to come and stay with him. It was for the canonization of Mother Seton. Bernadette went with me. We met the girl that was healed from Leukemia. She was nine years old and her mother prayed to Mother Seton. Her life was saved by a miracle. The girl grew up and got married and had two children. Her son was about twenty and got beaten up. He was in the hospital but didn't receive a miracle. He died. She was also divorced years later.

The year we went to Rome was 1975. Every 25 years they open the door for the whole year and then seal it again for 25 more. In St. Peters Basilica, it was so crowded we had to wait about 72 hours to get in. We visited the catacombs and all the places that my mother and I went to four years ago.

When we returned home it was midnight and raining. I called to tell my brother I would be at his house in the morning to get my mother. My sister-in-law said to come right now. I said it was raining. She said she had an umbrella. I went to get her that night. The reason she was so anxious, my mother kept calling me all week. She didn't want to spend another night without any sleep. My mother talked to her in Polish and she didn't understand any of it. At first she kept asking for "pic". In Polish it's drink of water or other drink. My sister-in-law thought she said a peach. She didn't have anything in the house so she asked my brother what to do. He knew a little bit of Polish and told her what it was. She got her a drink and learned a little bit of Polish that week.

Summer came quickly. I closed the store for two months and we traveled: Virginia Beach, Ocean City, Wildwood. It was so much fun. My sister went with us. She was a lot of fun and Bernadette, my mother and sister got along the whole trip. I'm glad that we could spend so much time together. When we got home, my mother was ready to go again. She was like a two year old and called me "mom". It is so sad to see anyone go senile. They don't get their memory back.

We spent one more memorable summer together. Then at Thanksgiving she started to fail. By Christmas eve, we couldn't have Wigilia. Everyone came to wish her Merry Christmas. Not all at once. All day, every few hours, someone came. They didn't want to tire her out too much. Lynda came late and brought her children. One had a little toy and showed it to my mother. She didn't just look at it, she grabbed it and wouldn't give it back. That made the kids cry because they didn't get it back until the next day.

My grandson, Bryan, was seven years old and he played on my mother's bed after school. He lined up all his toy soldiers and cars on the foot of her bed knocking them over and putting them back again and again. She was happy because he spent so much time with her. Four years is a lot of time. I was learning to play the piano and she thought I was playing for her. She would sing in Polish and French and tried to dance when sitting in her wheel chair. Each day she got weaker. The Doctor said if she got worse we would have to take her to the hospital. That night we did and she died about an hour later. I am glad that she was happy until the last. Good thing I was healthy enough to take care of her and not put her in a nursing home. With the help of Bernadette and Bryan we did it. The family helped whenever we needed them. They loved her too.

When a person is bed-ridden and can't get to church, a priest comes to the house once a month to bring them Holy Communion. One day he asked why I didn't put my mother in a nursing home. I told him when I was a baby she didn't put me in an orphanage, so I won't put her in a nursing home. Today I am thankful that I didn't. I wish she could have lived to be a hundred or more. She was 76 when she died.

The ladies from St. Ann's group in our church wanted me to come to their meetings. I was a member for about ten years but wasn't able to attend their monthly meetings or work at the dinners and dances in our church. After my mother passed away, they knew I had time to join them. They needed help. It's the Polish Women's Alliance. Every four years they held a convention. It was in another State and lasted five days. I always paid my dues every month by dropping the books at the financial secretary's house. She came to my house and brought all her books, explaining them to me. I didn't know she was ill. A few months later she died. God works in mysterious ways. I think He was setting me up to take her place. I had to do it. It's over thirty years now.

Soon after taking that job I was asked to join the Polish choir in our church. I didn't sing on the choir since I was in the 8th grade. My voice wasn't good enough to try for the American Idol but when you sing in a group, you blend in with all the other voices and it's not bad.

Our first convention was in Dearborn, Michigan. We spent the first day for registration. Then we have a few hours to get acquainted with the members from 14 districts from all different parts of the United States. I think we had 384 members attending. The second day we went to mass and had our banquet that evening. If the Mayor and Governor of that town can spare the time, they are invited. If they can't they send someone to represent them. On the third day, we went to mass and started the meetings. The fourth day we are busy attending the parties. The candidates have to get people to vote for them. The fifth day we have the elections for all the officers. In between the meetings we get to go to a dinner or some other event.

We were at a dinner in a church hall. There were priests at the dinner and they had some entertainment. One of the ladies came into the hall in a bathing suit. It was a one piece, down to the ankles from the 1920's. She said it was her grandmother's. She found it in the attic in a trunk. She was the mother of "Hot Lips" who played in MASH with Alan Alda on television. Another lady had a daughter that played the part of Dr. Margaret on "General Hospital" on TV soap operas. That was 1978.

Another trip to Europe. This one for the canonization of Bishop John Neumann. My roommate was a good friend. We were both members of the Third Order of St. Francis of Assissi. Her daughter wouldn't go on a plane and Bernadette wouldn't fly. My friend was the mother of the Monsignor at St. Anthony parish. She was 87 years old and they told me that I wouldn't enjoy the trip with anyone that age. We were as close as mother and daughter. Every Wednesday we went to her house to say the rosary, about six of us ladies. I had the best trip with her. She made the hours fly by on the plane, 9 and a half hours that is. I think we had 375 people on our plane. We left at midnight so everyone fell asleep. Everyone but her. She sang songs, talked, told jokes and prayed all night. Her son woke up and said: "Mom, you kept everyone up all night." She was so sorry but he said he was only kidding. His friends said they enjoyed it. The trip was planned by Cardinal Shehan and Archbishop Borders. They were close friends of hers too. When they had a meeting every month, they met at her house. After the meeting she would cook some Polish dish for them.

It's a small world. Every day someone called and came to our hotel to meet her son's friends. They had a suite and every night we met there. One night we met the vice president of the Coca Cola company and his daughter. Next day the Director of the Catholic University in Rome joined us for dinner, which the Cardinal had for the whole group. I fixed her hair which she always wore in a bun. I curled it and put it in a hair net. Everyone was surprised when we walked in. They said she looked 20 years younger. She went on all the tours and stayed up until 2 or 3 am talking. I fell asleep and she was still talking when I woke up after an hour or so. I didn't miss a thing on that trip, as a matter of fact I did more. She never got tired. She was too excited about meeting Pope Paul VI. She was a living saint. I learned a lot more about religion from her. I thought I learned a lot in school and at home. There is always more.

When we got home the Pope died. Pope John Paul I was elected. Thirty days later he died. Pope John Paul II was elected.

When Bryan was 12 years old we took a trip cross country. It was the year Elvis Presley died. We were passing by Graceland. It was crowded so we didn't stop to see the inside. We visited a lot of museums and churches, the Hearst mansion, and stopped in Reno to play slots one day. We saw President Eisenhower's library and it was a very educational trip. We reached Los Angeles airport and Bryan was asleep in the back of the van. When he woke up, Bernadette said: "Happy Birthday, Bryan, your present is taped to the window." He opened up an envelop with a birthday card and a ticket to Hawaii. He thought it was a joke. She said to look out the window. There was a tower that brings all the planes in for a safe landing. We just had time to board the plane. It was close to my birthday, so I had a ticket too. We spent a week in

Honolulu, Hawaii and Kona and Hilo. We saw what happened at Pearl Harbor. When we drove to Diamond Head, the gate was closing. Bryan and Bernadette had to crawl through the gate as it was closing. Another couple didn't make it. On our way down the mountain we stopped at the guard-house and told them the couple was locked in. They got them out. We had to take a small plane to Hilo. We rented a car and drove from one end of the island to the other end. You don't have to go back to get a plane. They have one at the other end. On the way was a coffee plantation and a pineapple one. Before we got on the plane, we visited a gift shop and bought some souvenirs. There was also a restaurant near a volcano, "The Volcano House". Luckily it didn't erupt while we were there. It was scary seeing the bubbles on the edge of it. I didn't go near it but Bryan and Bernadette walked near it. I still remember how sweet the pineapples tasted. The coffee came in different flavors. We flew back to Honolulu. Then on to Los Angeles.

We had to drive home in time for Bryan to go to school. We only stopped in Las Vegas for one day. I got home just in time for me to do my laundry, go to the beauty shop and pack my suitcase. My birthday present also included a trip to see the Passion Play in Ober Ammergau. They have it every ten years. No one can be in the play except the people that were in that town. They had the black plague and so many people died. All the survivors asked God to spare them, and if they lived, they promised to put on the Passion play in thanksgiving. They have kept their promise since then.

We had to stay in private houses, not enough hotels for tourists. In the house we stayed, the children slept in a tent in their yard. When we awoke the couple had breakfast on the table. When we left to see the play, they gave us a ticket for lunch and dinner in a restaurant near the theatre. When we got back it was dark. I walked my friend to her house and forgot what house I was staying in. When I looked up and down the street, I saw a light blinking on and off in one house. I guess the couple must have expected someone getting lost, so they thought of the lights. I went to the house and it was the right one. It was worth the trip to see the Passion play.

Right down the street, there was a shop. The man that owned it, made everything himself. He was very talented. There was a military camp nearby and all the soldiers shopped there. He was kept busy. The rest of the trip was a blur. We went to a crystal factory. When we got back on the bus, the guide counted the people to make sure everyone was on the bus. A lady was standing up in the aisle talking and when the guide went to the back, she moved and the guide came back and counted her again. I thought someone was missing but the driver left before I could check. By the time I got to the guide and told her she might have counted wrong, we were on the beltway and couldn't go back for 20 minutes. A lady was missing. When we reached her, she looked as if she would faint. She hugged and kissed the bus driver, thanking him for coming back for her. If you miss the bus, it is your responsibility to get to the next destination.

On a trip to an island we missed the boat. Rather we got on the wrong boat. The guide told us to wait for her before we got on the boat. After touring the island, we went to get on the boat. The guide wasn't there but we saw our guide from America getting on the boat so we thought the plans had changed. We followed her and the boat was about a block from the shore, when we saw the guide shaking her fist toward us. Then we heard the Captain on the loud speaker telling us that we were on the wrong boat and had to get off at the next stop and wait for the right boat to take us back. When we got off the boat, there was no place to sit down, no shade from the hot sun. It took two hours before we got the right boat. After that we made sure we listened to the right guide. The bus driver could not drive back to pick us up.

Time to go home, too foggy. We had to stay until the next morning. Weather was fine and we left. Had to stop in London. A satellite broke in pieces and we couldn't leave until the next day. We didn't mind. They gave us a free room in a hotel, free breakfast and dinner.

A bus tour to London, all free. Next day we reached New York. They offered us a free room but we wanted to get home so we took a smaller plane and went home. That was a great summer.

The store was not as good at making a profit as when I started 35 years ago. I was thinking of closing the store. All these years I did not get robbed. I should have closed when I thought of it. Fate did it for me. I just put some money in an envelope and a man came in with his child. One of my regular customers. He saw me putting the money away. Usually I'm faster than that and don't let anyone see me. He acted so nervous and rushed out of the store before buying anything. He acted too suspicious. About fifteen minutes later a man walked in backwards. When he turned around he had a kerchief tied over his face. But he had the same pants and shirt the other man wore who came in with the child. I thought he was joking when he pulled out a gun. He stood there pointing the gun at me and didn't say a word. Probably didn't want me to hear his voice. I told him I know what he wanted. I stooped down to get some money but it was a few thousand dollars, so I changed my mind. Finally he said, give me the envelope. I knew he had to be the same man. I told him I had the money in the other room. When I started to go in the other room he clicked the gun and I thought he would shoot me. My sister-in-law gave me a statue of St. Theresa and I put it on a shelf near the door to the other room. As I walked past the shelf, I looked at St. Theresa and asked her to help me. My mind was working fast. What am I going to tell him when I don't come back with the money. I remembered I always told my customers if anyone tried to rob me, I had a rifle in the other room and I would blow their brains out all over the store. He must have remembered that too. I hid behind a wall and grabbed the phone and started to call the police. My grandson Bryan was in the room and asked me why I was calling the police. I told him to get out of the doorway. He said nobody was in the store. The man must have thought I was crazy and run out of the store. A girl came in and I asked her if she saw anyone run out of the store. She said she did and she knew him but she wouldn't be a witness. I didn't blame her, he might have hurt her if she did. By the time the police got there he could have been out of town. They asked me how much money I gave him, I said nothing. He told me I was taking a chance on him shooting me. I asked him if he would have given me back the money and he said "No". Then I said I was glad I did not give the money to the thief. It was bad enough to stand there with a gun being pointed at you.

Bernadette was working all night and she was upstairs asleep. The noise woke her up and she came down. After she heard what happened, she closed the store and said I didn't have to work any more. What can I get into now?

I still had two years to wait for my social security. I did save a little money for a rainy day. With Bernadette paying the bills, I only needed a little income. So I lived on the interest and didn't have to spend the money. If I did spend it, there would be no interest for me to live on. I sold her the store and the house next door. That helped me to live a little longer without getting a job. She loved to travel and didn't want me to go to work so I could travel with her. That worked for me. For a while, we were the three musketeers: Bryan, Bernadette and I.

There were times when we couldn't go together. She couldn't get off from work when I planned a trip to Portugal. A day before I left her dog got lost. The church we were going to visit, was where St. Anthony was buried. He was the one we prayed to when someone or something got lost. She gave me money to have a mass said so her dog would be found. The next day her dog was found before I left. I gave the money for the mass in thanksgiving for the dog being found. St. Anthony really works fast.

When we reached the shrine of Our Lady of Fatima, we couldn't see the tree that our Lady was seen in by the three children. The people took pieces of the branches and there was nothing left. They put a few branches on the spot where the tree was, so we could see where the Blessed Mother was. They built a beautiful basilica and when it was done, they buried the two younger children at the foot of the side altar on the right side. Lucia lived to be almost 100 years old. We did not meet Lucia. She was in a convent where no one could see her. Only one lay person ever saw her. Lucia had a message for him. He was the president of the Blue Army. They have a replica of the shrine in Washington, New Jersey.

When we visited the house Lucia was born in, her sister was sitting outside. We met her and I talked to her.

From Fatima we took a plane to Paris, France. A priest took us to the church where St. Vincent de Paul is in a glass coffin over the main altar. You go up the stairs on the right and come down another stairway on the left.

I was looking forward to see the church that St. Theresa saw the Blessed Mother in. It was right around the corner of our hotel. I got up early in the morning and walked around the corner and saw scaffolds all around the church. It was closed for renovations. What a disappointment that was for me. I had just read the book about the life of St. Theresa and wanted to see the chair and touch it. This was the chair that the Blessed Mother was sitting in when St. Theresa saw her.

I did not have time to charter a bus to see the convent she was in. When I asked the guide if he could help me, he said "yes". But I had to have 25 people and I only got thirteen to go. Everyone was sad and went up to their room. Another lady and I were in the lobby and I looked at the desk clerk and thought he might be able to help. I asked him and he said he had a friend that drives a bus. He called him and we did it. He said only thirteen would be fine. We only had to pay half of what the other guide wanted. I went upstairs and rapped on the door of each person that wanted to go. Each one was praying for me to make the trip. Sometimes your prayers are answered.

The bus driver couldn't speak any English and I couldn't speak French. The clerk told him where we were going. At noon he stopped at a restaurant to eat lunch. We didn't get off the bus, we were in a hurry because we had to get back for a dinner and a boat ride. I showed him a bag full of snacks, a nun had enough for all of us. We had a bag of chips, peanut butter crackers, a few oranges, some cookies. A very tasty lunch. Then I showed him the time I had written on a piece of paper and waved my hand to tell him to hurry. He caught on. We visited the church and the convent. We also visited the house St. Theresa was born in and the hills she climbed with her grandfather, when she was a little child. We did get back in time and we went to the dinner that the first guide had arranged for us. He was the guide who wanted to charge us more money for the bus. He promised to make it a special dinner. It was cold cuts and cheap wine which made the people sick.

One threw up several times. One girl was so sick she couldn't go on the boat trip. She spent the time in the hotel room trying to get well. I was not able to remember getting on the boat. When I got better, I saw the statue of Liberty and said "when did we get home?"

I thought we were in New York. Then I saw that it was much smaller than ours. At first I thought it shrank. I must have said that aloud, they all laughed at me. I wasn't drunk. I only had two small glasses of wine.

After Paris we went to Lourdes, France, where St. Bernadette saw the Blessed Mother. They have the Stations of the Cross in back of the church. The last one is on top of a mountain. I could hardly make it and was going to turn back, when I saw a group of older people. Some about ninety years old were going up, so I kept on going up to the top. It was easy coming down. I ran all the way. I just made it in time for the Mass. It started to rain just when the procession started. We walked in the rain, reciting the rosary. Everyone had a lighted candle and the flame did not go out even though the rain drops were falling on them.

We took a bath in the water that comes from the spot that St. Bernadette dug in the ground. She was told to do so by the Blessed Mother. When you go into the baths, you have to take off your clothes and put on a gown. There is a bathtub you walk into. The water is cold. A lady is on each side and they take your arms, one on each side, and they tell you to pray. They sit you down and you lay back not putting your head in the water only up to your shoulders. They get you up and you stand there until they put your lingerie on. You can't touch your clothes until you get on a bench near the door. No towel, I thought how can I get dressed all wet like that. I wasn't wet, I was very dry. Even my nylons went on without drying my feet. We walked out of there feeling like we were wearing haloes on our heads.

The people that get healed when they go there, come back every summer as volunteers. They help to wheel the people from the hospital to the grotto where the Blessed Mother appeared to St. Bernadette.

That night, the mattress on our bed was so bumpy, I didn't think I would sleep that night. As soon as my head touched the pillow, I felt no lumps and I slept all night.

The next day we walked to St. Bernadette's house, which was close to the hotel. They were so poor, they chewed on a limb from a tree to keep from being hungry.

Next stop was Rome. We had a guide take us to the Sistine chapel where Michelangelo painted the ceiling. When the group left we didn't see them. Another lady and I were left. I thought I knew my way out and told her not to worry. We took the wrong way and ended up in the basement where all the priceless pieces are. The guard showed us the door to the outside. Wrong door. We were in the back of the basilica and we were supposed to be in the front. We walked and walked for 30 minutes. Everyone else was in the room waiting for us. The guide should have counted the people before leaving the room. Like I do when I have my bus trips.

I chartered a bus the next day to see Brother Gino. He received the stigmata like St. Francis had in his hands and feet. Padre Pio died and told him he would be a stigmatist. It was only about a half hour from Rome. Brother Gino was trying to get boys to join the priesthood. There were about 60 boys in the school and 600 girls in the convent. I just talked seven people into going. It was a mini bus, more like a van. They put an extra seat in to fit everyone. We were in time for the Mass. Brother Gino was distributing Communion in the middle aisle. We were in that line. After the Mass everyone walked to a hall where you could write a note and give it to him. He couldn't speak English but one of the nuns translated for him. She told us her mother did not speak Italian. She went to confession and he heard her in Italian and she heard him talk to her in English. She asked him to pray for her son. He was leading a wild life. He told her not to worry, her son would change. He did for a better life. He went to school there and became a priest.

When it was my turn to shake hands with Brother Gino he pulled his hand away. I felt like I was a sinner and that was why but it was because he was in pain. When it eased up he did shake hands with me.

We had a man in a wheel chair in our group. He could not stand or talk. His two sisters took him on the trip, hoping for a miracle. He came close to brother Gino and said out loud: "He's a fake." Brother Gino blessed him and we left. The man talked after being blessed by Brother Gino. He said "Hello" to everyone. When we went to church, during mass, he stood up at the gospel and got out of his wheelchair.

On the road back the ladies asked if we smelled a heavenly fragrance. We didn't want to tell them because we thought they would imagine it. There is a statue of the Infant of Prague in a glass case in the church. Once a year the case is opened and a liquid foam oozes out of the foot of Jesus. The fragrance lasts until the next year.

It was July 4th and we were going to be back to the hotel just in time to see the fireworks. When we didn't see any, we thought there were no fireworks. It is an American holiday, not an Italian holiday. When we got home I had a job, babysitter. They weren't babies. Bryan was ten, Zachary was seven, Heather was six. Pat had an operation and couldn't go back to work for about six weeks. Bernadette took advantage of that time and talked them into a vacation. They went cross country and left the children with me. That's a good way to get closer to them. They came home in time for Zachary to receive his First Holy Communion.

There was a leak at three mile island and some people got a scare for awhile.

Bernadette took advantage of the time and talked Lynda into taking the children to Disney World in Florida. A group was organizing a trip to Rome for the canonization of Father Kolbe. Since I went for his beatification, I felt like I should go with them. A few people from our church also joined us.

One man with the group had a sore on his leg and the Doctor wanted to amputate. If they didn't he might die. He prayed to Father Kolbe for a cure. He didn't let them amputate his leg and it was cured. He still had his leg. He taught us how to do the chicken dance. He learned how to get around in Rome without getting lost. We took the subway to St. Paul Outside the Wall and then went shopping across from the Vatican. They had a shop there where all the bishops and priests shopped. He had a black suit and a ring that looked like a bishop's and the saleslady mistook him for a bishop. He got the VIP treatment in that shop.

I walked from the hotel to the Vatican by myself one day, I followed the street car that went past our hotel that way I didn't get lost. When I got to the same shop, I bought a bag full of medals. I had time so I took a walk to the Basilica—St. Peter's—and decided to go to the top of the dome. An elevator takes you about three stories up and you have to walk up 300 stairs to the top. I was half way when I ran out of breath. Carrying that heavy bag was not a good idea. I had to stop and rest three times before I reached the top of the dome. It was a beautiful view from there, you could see the Vatican gardens and the Swiss guards standing at the entrance.

Nobody could go into the gardens without a pass. We went in with a group one time. I didn't have any trouble coming down. When I got to the front of the Basilica, it was early. I sat on the steps and watched the men setting up the chairs for the next day, usually it is so crowded. That day hardly anyone was there. When I got back to the hotel, the TV was on in the lobby. I listened to the news and they said there was a bomb scare at the Vatican. No wonder the men working there left and probably thought I had a lot of faith in St. Peter because I didn't leave.

When I got back home our church asked for volunteers to work in the office answering the phones and I had the time so I worked a few days a week. I also stapled the weekly bulletin and little things that came up. One day the priest said he was going to dinner. If anyone called on the phone I was not to call him unless it was the Pope. It sounded like a joke. Someone called and said he was the Pope. I wrapped on the dining room door and told the priest. He got right up and answered. Good thing I talked nice and didn't say anything bad, it was the Pope. He was a personal friend of the priest.

A lady called and asked if there was anyone in the parish that could watch her bed-ridden mother at night. I called several women but they were all working elsewhere. Bernadette was working at the Post Office in the daytime but she had to sleep at night. The lady asked if she could do it just until someone else was found. Bernadette worked there until her mother died. She was a good patient and she slept all night and Bernadette could get her sleep in also. She only spoke Polish but they got along somehow. She asked me to go visit her. I went and talked to her in Polish. She was 99 years old but still had a good memory. When she was dying her daughter called and asked me to pray for her. I was saying my prayers at the time and was on the page that had a prayer for a person who was dying. When I finished my prayer, her daughter called and said she died peacefully. We were friends and after her mother died, we went out once a week when Bernadette could take us. She lived in a mansion and I thought she was a high society lady. I found out she only moved there a few years ago. She was from our neighborhood and her sister went to school with me.

Her husband lived next door to us before he married her. What a small world this is. She asked me to come to her house and listen to some tapes she had, religious ones. We could sit on the balcony and enjoy the view. It was summer time. I didn't have time then and she passed away before I could listen to the tapes.

She did give me one for Christmas. She even got Ben to come to her house. He had pigeons and she had a problem with them in her yard. She asked him if he could take care of it. He took a trap and put it in her yard. The pigeons walked into it and walked out of it. It was as if they didn't want to leave her.

While I was working in the rectory, when Father Ron finished his work, he would play music and sing in several different languages. It would make the time go faster. Before I knew it, it was time to go home. Best job I had yet.

The priest from Poland came to America in the summer to work in our church while the other priests took their vacation. Then they went back when school started. Most of them taught the seminarians in the universities. I had a bus trip to Atlantic City and invited our priest and the one from Poland to go with us. They were really impressed at seeing all the casinos, especially the Taj Mahal. It is so beautiful. The priest from Poland knew that I was taking a trip to Europe with Bernadette and my two grandsons. Bryan was 17 and Zachary was 13 years old. He said he knew the priest in Rome who was in charge of giving tickets to tourists to have an audience with the Pope. He said he would give me a letter to give to the priest when we arrived in Rome.

Another favor I did for him was to try to make an appointment with Joni, the girl who was in a wheel chair because when she was swimming she dove into the water and hurt her spine.

It paralyzed her. I found her phone number and called her. She wasn't home but her mother answered. When I told her that the priest wanted to meet her daughter she was sorry. Her daughter was traveling and wouldn't be home before the priest had to go home. She invited him to come to her house and she would give him some pictures to take back home and give to the teenagers in his church who were fans of Joni.

A new priest came to work in our church. He had a beautiful singing voice. He could have been famous if he chose to be on the stage. He chose to work for God. Some people came to our church just to hear him sing. He is in another church now but we see him when he comes for special celebrations or when we go to some other church where he is helping.

I was planning the trip to Europe. I saw an ad in the paper and it said if you become a member of the traveling club for $39 you can get plane tickets for a discount. You can take a guest. I became a member and so did Bernadette. That would buy us four tickets. Every day I called the club to find out the prices. One day it was $69 a person to go to Paris. That was cheap enough. You had to get the return tickets. The cheapest I could get was $500 and we had to go to England to get the plane. Before I ordered them, Bernadette came in from work and said someone there told her about an airline that was starting business and was charging $99 and you had to leave from Brussels. That was closer to where we would be and I ordered them. Then I saw an ad for a 15 day train pass for

$260 per person. The train went to fifteen different countries. We saved about $3,000 by buying the tickets through the club. It helped to buy a lot of souvenirs to bring back home.

I was watching TV and on the news they showed a plane crash and almost 200 people were killed. There were no survivors. I asked Bryan and Zachary if they still wanted to go. They said they could get killed on the street. Zachary had to go get something a block away. When he was coming back a man came out of the bar across the street and another man came out arguing with him. He pulled out a gun and shot the other man just as Zachary walked by. He wasn't hurt but said: "see grandma, he could have shot me".

So, on to Paris. We got off the plane and were told to make reservations at a hotel. They charged a $20 deposit. We got a cab to take us to the hotel. It was closed. We found out they closed for two months at that time for vacations. We did find two nice rooms on our own. No more reservations at the airport. They must know which hotels are closed and con you, unless you have traveled before and knew better.

Our hotel was close enough to the Eiffel Tower we could walk to it. Also Notre Dame and the Louvre where the Mona Lisa is displayed. We gave the boys $20 bills to take to the bank and change into francs. When I was there the first time I got one and a half francs for each dollar. They came back with four francs for a dollar. They caught on very fast in each country how to count the money. They bought so much we could hardly carry everything.

When they bought clothes they wore them. A sweater, a jacket, a hat etc. The first night we were getting ready for bed. Bernadette put her money in her socks to keep it safe. When she washed her socks she forgot to take the money out first and got all the bills wet. I took each one apart and laid them across the bed to dry. I rapped on the door to the boys' room and told them to come into our room to see something. I told them their aunt was so clean she even washed her money. I had them going for awhile and I couldn't hold it in any longer. I burst out laughing and they knew it was a joke. It was worth the look on their face.

We took the train to Rome. We had a ticket for a private compartment but when we had to go in, the people were in it and told us we were in the wrong one. It took so long to find the conductor and by the time he checked it out we were in Rome. The next train we took we told the people it was our compartment. They did not take advantage of us again.

We got a room across from the Vatican. The Pope was at the Castle Gondalfo. We found the convent where the priest was with the tickets. A nun answered the door and we asked her for the tickets. She said: "sorry, no tickets." I showed her the letter that I had gotten from the priest at home and she read it and took us to wait for the priest who had the tickets. When he came in, he also said no. After she gave him the letter, he then gave us four tickets. That must have been some letter.

The people that came from Poland stayed at the convent. They were only allowed to bring a few dollars with them and couldn't afford a hotel. They also ate their meals there. They were going to the castle in the morning on a bus. We planned to go with them. We missed the bus by a minute. You couldn't call a cab that early in the morning. We had to wait until one came by. We all prayed and one came down the street. When we reached the castle, the bus just got there before us. Zachary saw everyone holding their tickets. I thought they were postcards and left them at the hotel. The sister was at the gate. I told her I left the tickets at the hotel. She said: "so." But then she counted out four more and gave them to us. We just made it because once they close the gate, you can't get in.

The Pope had a Mass in the courtyard. After the Mass he took a picture with about twenty people. We were in the front of the group and can be seen clearly. The priest at home said to say hello to the Pope, but when he passed near me, I started to talk to him and the guard wouldn't let me get close. I started to yell but he couldn't hear me. It was just after he had gotten shot and they were guarding him closely. I think our priest told him later when he talked to the Pope on the phone that I tried to talk to him. He told the Pope that he had sent an angel but she didn't do her job.

We came back to Rome and they told us to go to some studio to get the picture. They didn't have it. Someone else told us to go to the Vatican studio. No pictures there either. I said to Bernadette that they must be at the convent where we got the tickets and sure enough they were. They were 8 x 10 and in color. There were four pictures left at only $5.00 each. We were in luck. One for each of us.

Zachary's sister in school put a map of Europe on the chalk board and showed the children where we had been. They didn't believe Zachary but when he showed them that picture they could see for themselves. He also bought enough medals for everyone in the class. Sister didn't mind him taking time off from school. It helped the whole class to learn geography the easy way.

We liked Rome so much we stayed five days. We took the train to Florence, Pisa, Assisi and Venice. We took the boat in Venice to St. Mark's square. I got a blister on my foot and couldn't wear my shoes. I didn't want to stay in the room, so I had a pair of bedroom slippers Zachary had. They were funny and big and made me look like Goofy in Disneyland. But I went out anyway.

I tried to take them to see Brother Gino but he was not at the church. He was going to the schools to talk to the boys about going to the seminary to become priests. We took the train to Switzerland, Austria and Holland. We saw Mozart's birthplace and shopped at the marketplace. We slept on a boat in Holland. Bernadette wanted to see if she could sleep on a boat if we ever took a cruise. We walked through Lichtenstein. They couldn't make up their mind whether to make it a part of Austria or Switzerland so they made it a country in itself. We took a ride to the top of the mountain in Switzerland. The chair lift we rode up in had a hole in the bottom. The boys weren't scared, they kept kicking the bottom making out it was falling apart. I found out later that one of them did fall down and the people in it were killed. Bernadette wasn't taking any chances. She stayed at the bottom and didn't go up with us. It was a beautiful view from the top. I don't know if I would go up again.

In Bonn, Germany, we went to Beethoven's birthplace. We looked for his grave at the cemetery. Bernadette found every place easy. After we asked directions, which weren't very good, she did a better job, especially at finding the street with all the shops. There was a lot more to carry when they finished shopping. I didn't buy much. After seven trips I had enough at home. So I helped to carry their bags. In Berlin the streets were so clean. Workers were sweeping the street, not machines. In Munich we saw the clock that has the statues going around every hour. There were a lot of tourists walking up to see the clock, we didn't have to look for it.

I wanted to see where Grace Kelly lived. We took the train to Monaco. Bernadette and I were tired so we sat on a bench and the boys went to the wall which wasn't very high, and were looking at something so long we thought it must be really good. It was an eye full. There was a huge Olympic pool, where they trained for the Olympics. Next to it was a beach full of girls—topless. It was too far for them to see clearly but they saw enough to keep them there. When the girls came up on the boardwalk they had to put on a top. The boys waited for nothing. We saw the road that Grace Kelly had the car accident on that killed her. When we wanted to go into one shop, we couldn't go in. They just cleaned the floors and shined them up and they were still wet. They were expecting the Prince to go shopping in their shop.

We had two days left on the train pass. If we went to Brussels we would be close to the airport. We got off the train and got a room. The last one in that part of town. We paid for it without seeing it first. A rickety elevator took us to the third floor to the rooms. We all said no way can we sleep here. There were dead roaches on the shelves. We went back down but couldn't get our money back unless somebody else came in for the room. A couple came in and said they couldn't find a room anywhere. We said here is one. We got our money back. We did not know they had two stops in Brussels. We stopped where they had a street called the Red Light. We soon found out it was like Baltimore's BLOCK. We went to buy souvenirs and there were filthy objects on sale. We walked down the street and topless girls were near the window looking for business. We walked down that street fast. Right on to the train station. We went to the next stop which was much nicer. We got a nicer room and their street had ritzy restaurants and violin players instead of the girls.

In the morning we started to look for the train station since we forgot the name of the street. We asked a man but he couldn't speak English. Bernadette tried French but he didn't understand. I tried Polish and he was from Poland. He knew where it was. The train took us right into the airport. How convenient that was. Imagine all the cab fares and bus fares we saved by getting that pass. We traveled through eight countries. There was France, Italy, Switzerland, Lichtenstein, Austria, Germany, Monaco and Belgium.

My grandsons thanked us for the trip and said they might not be able to travel like that again. They do a lot of traveling in our own country, the good old USA.

Before we left on that trip, my friend had a stroke and was in the hospital. I told her I would bring her the holy water from Lourdes. Two days after we got home I took it to her. She died the next day. I wasn't glad that she died but I was glad that she didn't have to suffer any more. They fed her through a tube in her stomach. She couldn't eat by herself. It must have been painful. She pulled it out and they tied her hands to the bed so she wouldn't do it again. It was about two years that she suffered. That was long enough.

I went a few days a week to see my sister who was sick. She couldn't do much any more.

Ben was trying to get back with us again. One day Bernadette and I were eating at a restaurant. He came over to our booth and sat next to Bernadette and said: "how about a kiss for your father?" She said: "I don't kiss any dirty old men." He had a sad look on his face and went back to his table. She asked me and Lynda if we knew him. I said: "I think that was your father." She didn't hear him say that. We didn't see him for many years and he aged, got gray and grew a beard. I half recognized him. She went over to his table and asked his brother if it was him. Then she said that she was sorry that she talked that way to him. He kept on going to the same restaurant hoping I would talk to him. After two years, she took us to his house and said she had to pick up something. She came out of the house and said for us to come in for just a few minutes. He cleaned the house and wanted us to see it. Lynda and I finally gave in and first thing I said as I walked in the door, was that we were in a hurry, can only stay a few minutes. It was close to valentine's day so he gave Bernadette some money to take us out to dinner. She took us to the same place which was only $15 each. Smart.

Since Bernadette was working night shift it was hard for her to drive me up to my sister's house. Ben offered to take me. He was busy with his pigeons all day, he had thousands of them, but he never complained. He said he wasn't going to give up trying to get back this time. When I went to work in the rectory, the priest said it was not right to be mad at someone all those years. Bernadette said he was a changed person. Soon I started to forgive him. He met the grandchildren, five of them. The oldest one was 23 years old. He missed seeing them grow up. It felt good to have someone to lean on again. When there was a problem, he helped straighten it out. Even my sister took his side. She always did. That is why he liked her and helped me to take care of her.

We got remarried after 35 years of divorce. I was going to have a quiet wedding but Lynda said: "if a daughter can wear her mother's wedding dress, why can't a mother wear her daughter's?" It just fit me. Ben's brother was a member of the VFW club and rented that hall. His sister had a Polish trio playing at an affair and said they were good so she hired them for us. The priest looked at the date book in the rectory and gave us a free date. Our friends asked where the wedding would be and we didn't have to send any invitations. Jerry was the Best Man and Bernadette and Lynda were bridesmaids. Everything worked out by itself. I didn't have to do anything but show up at the church. Ben's sister said it felt like I wasn't gone those 35 years. It didn't feel like it to me either.

Years ago a fortune teller told me I would get married again and have a big wedding and have five children. I only had three but Ben had two girls so that made five. I forgot about that fortune teller until it came true.

When we got married, I moved. Before that, Bernadette, Lynda and I would go shopping and have dinner. Ben was busy with his pigeons so he didn't mind. Every morning Ben and I went to Mass. I still worked a few days in the rectory and went to my sister's house to help take care of her. She was getting weaker and couldn't do much. Her adopted daughter was working and couldn't take care of her all week. Ben was busy building a bedroom to our house. He did all the work himself except for the roof. He had to have help for that.

My sister got worse and her daughter couldn't take care of her any longer. Ben said I could bring her to our house. I was glad I didn't have to drive back and forth. The traffic was getting worse.

I had to stop working at the rectory. I still had the bus trips. Bernadette took care of my sister when I had the trips.

My sister enjoyed watching Ben and his helper finish up the bedroom. They did a good job. She kept telling them to do this or that. She took the job of supervisor. When they finished, she missed her job. It was a large bedroom with a walk in closet. Before I put the furniture in we used it as a dining room. It was near to Christmas and the whole family came to celebrate Wigilia on Christmas eve. We had two large tables and everyone could sit at the table at one time. We had to take turns when the dining room was too small for everyone to sit at one time. After dinner we sang Christmas carols. After that my sister got weaker. She could hardly make it from the bed to the potty chair, next to the bed. She was with me for seven months. One day she slipped. I had to call an ambulance. Ben was strong but even he couldn't help me pick her up. The ambulance took her to the hospital and she had to have a brace put on her leg. I could no longer take care of her and had to put her in a nursing home. It was within walking distance of our home so I could get there every day. I kept praying for her to get better so that I could take her home again. She was there ten months and got pneumonia. Two months later she passed away. It was during Lent and our church was celebrating forty hours devotion. I didn't think they had a funeral during forty hours, but they did.

The choir sang during the funeral. They were already in church for the Devotion. My sister was a very strict Catholic and I am sure she is in heaven. Just in case, I still pray for her soul. I was lucky to have such a good sister. The rest of the family were good too. We were a close family. We still celebrate the Wigilia on Christmas eve, with our own families. It is so many now we rent a hall about a week before and everyone attends. All the little ones are grown and have children of their own. I think we had about 72 there last year. It keeps getting bigger. We get together more than once a year. There are weddings, 1st Holy Communions, special birthdays. Ben was 80 years old and we rented a hall to celebrate it.

Bernadette and I attended the PWA (Polish Women's Alliance) convention. It was in Secaucus, New Jersey. We had a day free at the end of the convention and took a ride into New York. We wanted to see a Broadway show but couldn't get tickets. They are sold out about a year ahead. We had lunch and went back to the hotel to pack and go home. I had taken the job at the convention to take the minutes. When I got home I had 30 days to listen to the tapes I brought home with me and had to type them up and send them back to Park Ridge, IL. Bernadette typed them for me. Ben helped by fixing his own meals during that time. It saved me a lot of time to get the minutes together. The two most important jobs at the convention are Chairman and Recording Secretary.

The next convention, four years later, Bernadette took the job of elections chairman. She had to take care of the machines that we vote on and see that no one votes twice. We vote for the new President, Secretary General, nine Directors, Treasurer etc. The PWA is an insurance company. They have members all over the world. Over a million members.

We have 257 members in our group, St. Ann's in Holy Rosary church. Every year on Mother's day we have a breakfast after Mass and whoever sells the most insurance is chosen as Queen and gets a crown. I won it one year. I sold a total of $450,000 of insurance. Most were from my family. My grandson's wife was due to have a baby the day I had to leave for the convention. My great grandson was born about an hour before I left. Now I have five grandchildren and seven great grandchildren and all are members. When they reach 15 years old, they can go to the children's convention. One year they went to Poland. They brought back video tapes and showed them to us at one of our seminars. My family was not on that trip. The ones that were did a good job showing the tapes and talking about the trip.

My grandson, Bryan, went when it was held in Orchard Lake. That is the seminary where boys go to study for the priesthood. He didn't go to the seminary later. They learn a lot about their Polish heritage and the PWA. It is not all study. They visited other places of interest. When they came home they wrote a report and read it to us at our seminars. We hope when they get older, they will continue to keep up the work their parents and grandparents started over 100 years ago. Some of them have started to take an interest in the groups and have become officers in their groups.

On one of my bus trips I celebrated my birthday. Ben and his cousin were on that trip. It was to Atlantic City. The casino was the Resorts. We were in front of the casino and Ben and Joe noticed the girls that worked there were handing people a card. They told me to get one. It was a chance to play the slots in a tournament. They wouldn't participate. After I played the slots along with 950 other people, they called ten names and I was one of them. Only eight showed up and we played again. I got the highest score and won $1,000. They took my picture and gave me the cash. There was a sheepish look on Ben and his cousin's face.

Ben got too busy with his pigeons and couldn't go on the trips with me. He helped me by driving to the bus and donating prizes for our raffle on the bus. Some were nice, some weren't. He shopped in an antique shop a lot. A week before Mother's day, Bernadette came to our house and said they were selling a shop in Highlandtown. We went to see if we could find any bargains. I found some things and so did Ben. It would have cost us $300 for the items we picked out. I was talking to the lady that owned the shop and she said that if someone would give her $1,000 she would sell everything in the shop. I went over to Ben and said we are about to pay $300 for a few things, would you like to have everything in the shop for $700 more? He said: "you're kidding." I told him the lady was serious. He asked me if I wanted a nice Mother's Day present. I said: "with pleasure." I thought it was all that we could see. After we paid her, she picked up the curtains that covered boxes full of items under the table, boxes in the back room, jewelry in her desk drawers. She gave them all to us. It took us three trips to clean out the store. We had a pick up truck and a van. There was an oil painting of Greece about 5 x 7 feet, three Barbie dolls in gowns about three foot high. There were two complete sets of dinnerware like new packed in a box. My dining room, bedroom and our porch were full. Ben said I had two weeks to clean up the boxes. I told the family to come up every day and take what they liked. Bernadette filled up her car for two weeks. She came every day. I took about 200 prizes for my bus trips. There was a rosary among the jewelry. It was from Greece. It looked very expensive. I used to pray on it every day.

One of the hand painted pictures from the store was signed by an artist that must be well known. I read an article about him in the Sunday papers. I haven't found out if it was an expensive painting or not. It must have been worth over $50,000 or more. What a bargain that was.

Ben wouldn't go to Poland with me so he paid for Bernadette's ticket and she went with me. She wanted to see where my mother lived. We went to the town and I expected to see the farm with cattle and chickens etc. What we did see were new houses that my cousins built on the property. She did meet the cousins and some of the children. One of them had a daughter that looked just like my granddaughter. My closest cousin looked like me. Her son looked like my brother.

We were supposed to meet the President of Poland. My cousin told me we would not. When we got to the President's house, they told us only three people were allowed to see him. Bernadette was disappointed because she was looking forward to meeting him. I don't think she will go with that group again.

We had a lot of elderly people in the group. They could just about make it when we went to see the Eye of the Ocean. The bus drove us half way up the mountain. Then a horse pulled a wagon full of people about ¾ths of the way. Then everyone had to walk to the top. I was in good shape then and it was hard for me to walk all the way. I can imagine how the older people felt. One lady couldn't take it and they called for a car to come up and take her back.

We were traveling with a Cello player and went to hear her play in different cities. We had no idea of doing that when we signed up for the trip. It did give us a chance to see some places we wouldn't have seen without her. It was a good thing she had to go without us when we were half way through the trip. It gave us some time to visit with my cousins. One part of the trip I liked was seeing the birthplace of Pope John Paul II. He lived in an apartment on the 2nd floor. From his bedroom window he could see a church. It was next door to his building. He was always close to the church.

My cousin took us to see Chopin's birthplace. It was not on the list of places the group was going to see.

We had a movie camera with us and took pictures of all the houses and people and showed them to the family when we got home.

We went with the group to meet Cardinal Glemp at his residence. He shook hands with everyone and when he finished, I shook his hand and told him that the priest from our church said he knew him and to say hello. I said that I was supposed to say it in Rome two years ago when I was on a tour there. He thought that was funny. I did not get close enough in Rome because there were about 65 priests, bishops, and a few cardinals at the church. The people in the group asked me what I said to make the Cardinal laugh so much. When I told them they laughed too.

Bernadette took a picture when he was shaking my hand and didn't show it to me until Mother's day. She had it enlarged and surprised me with it. This was my 8th trip. I don't know if I will go on any more trips. If I do it will be for the canonization of Sister Marie Angela Truszkowska. I have a relic of her on a holy picture and for 21 years I recited the prayers for my eyes to get better. I have had cataracts, glaucoma and macular degeneration for 21 years. My vision is getting worse. I had one cataract operated on. The other one is still to be done. Unless a miracle happens, that's what I have been praying for all these years. Whether it does or not, if she gets canonized, I will go to Rome if I can make the trip.

It was Thursday and Bernadette was working. After work she was going to pick me up for our weekly dinner and shopping. Lynda couldn't go that day. Ben was busy putting 500 pigeons in the crates for the next day. Someone called and he had to have them ready. When she got to our house he was only half done. It was a hot day and he looked very tired. When she saw him, she told me we will be late going out. She had to help him. By the time they finished, we were hungry. Instead of going somewhere fancy, we went to a fast food place. Since we had to go grocery shopping we went to the one across from the grocery store.

After eating and relaxing, she was tired too. We went to the grocery store, and as we walked in there was no one in line to buy tickets for the mega millions lottery. I bought five tickets and she bought four. Usually I bought ten, but Ben told me to buy them in two places instead of one. Wrong advice. I took a few minutes to count my change. Those minutes must have made a big difference. Then she bought the four tickets. That was all the money she had at the time. We went home and waited for the numbers to be called the next day. I didn't win. The news on TV said someone bought the winning ticket but didn't call in yet. I called and asked her if she won anything. She had gone to dinner and a movie with a friend. As she was sitting in the restaurant, her friend said that someone has the winning ticket. She couldn't remember all the winning numbers but had them written down at home. She remembered "1, 2, 3". When Bernadette looked at the ticket when she bought it she remembered she had those numbers. Then, she said to herself: "I might as well throw this one away." She didn't. When she got to her friend's house, they checked the numbers. She had all of them. I called her again and she said she won $5,000. I said that that was good and it was better than I did.

The next day I had a bus trip to Atlantic City. When we were on the bus I asked everyone if they had won anything on the lottery. She raised her hand halfway but nobody could see her. I told them that Bernadette had won $5,000. On TV they said whoever has the ticket is losing $40,000 interest each day or week if they didn't turn in the ticket. Then it said that the grocery store where we shopped had sold the winning ticket and it was bought by one of two women. One of them had to have it. When they said what time it was bought, I knew it had to be her because it wasn't me. She still wouldn't tell me. She was trying to think of how to invest the money before anyone could start giving her the wrong advice.

My granddaughter-in-law who she was living with at the time suspected her to be the winner and called me up. We put all the clues together and waited for her to tell us.

Finally the next day, we were going to the post office where she worked. There were five of us including my grandson Bryan, his wife and his daughter. It was a little car and we just fit the five of us in it. At first I told her I wasn't going because I was too sick. She said: "I will take you to the Doctor." I said it was nothing the Doctor could do and I told her I was worried because if she did win and someone found out, they would hurt her trying to get the ticket away from her. She said that I was worse than a little kid making things up in your mind. So she told me I would feel better if I went with her.

When we got to the Post Office she parked across the field at a restaurant and told us to get something to eat while she went to the Post Office to fill out some papers. We got something and waited for about a half hour. I would have parked in front of the Post Office but not her. She walked across the field. Finally she came back and said to sit down, she had something to show me. It was the winning ticket. My granddaughter in law and I burst out crying tears of relief. We were both so worried about her it was nerve wracking. After we got done telling her how she made us feel bad by keeping us in suspense for so long, we went to her friend's farm and greenhouse and she bought a few plants. She didn't realize how small her car was and we had to hold some on our laps and some on the floor next to our feet. When we got to Bryan's house, my ankle had a dent in it. It took a while before it got better.

We then went to my brother's house. He is an accountant and she asked him a few things before she called the lottery.

What a relief it was to see her turn over the ticket to the lottery. My son Jerry worked in the same building as the lottery. He was on the floor above. The lottery people called him down. When he got down there, they said to him: "I guess you know why your sister is here?" And Jerry said: "I guess she won some money in the lottery." They asked him if he saw on TV how much the amount was on the mega millions and Jerry replied that it was a lot. When they said the amount was $183 million and that Bernadette had won that amount, Jerry said: "Holy Shit!" I said to myself what are people going to think of a mother who teaches her children to talk like that. I did not teach him to talk like that. When children grow up they pick up those words.

Bernadette and Jerry grew up trying to compete with each other. When he got a job, she tried to get a better one. They have been at it for years. Now she turned around and said: "Let him top this."

We went to the Governor's office and TV reporters took our picture with the Governor and it was on television on the news. By her winning, the State got almost a large part of the winnings.

Lynda, Pat and I went to California with her to be on the Jay Leno show on TV (which Jerry arranged but couldn't go). A lot of people sent her hundreds of letters. She got some of them but not all. They were thrown away and she didn't get them all. Phone calls day and night. Jerry handled a lot of them for her. Most people wanted a million dollars or more. If she gave it to them it would not be enough for even a little part of them. There were hundreds and she didn't get that much, after taxes and the State's share.

She gave a lot of donations to the churches that she was close to. I can't count all the other charities and she is still donating to them. She couldn't even give the family millions because of the gift tax. She could give them annual checks of $11,000. That is better because they would have spent it foolishly and not have it. This way she helps them every year.

My grandson's wife had a baby and it was a very expensive one. He was only one pound five ounces. The hospital bill was over $300,000. The insurance didn't cover it all so she paid the rest. Then she sent the grandson to a school to learn audio/video and lighting in hopes of him getting a better job. He has three children now. When they go to college, he will need it.

She gave me some money and I gave a check to my family and then sent a check to all my cousins in Poland and a few churches and orphanages. When I was done sharing it with everyone it was all gone. Now I am hoping to win the lottery. There are so many people that need help and I could help them if I win. Gives you a good feeling when you help someone in need.

We didn't need it but she splurged one day and bought two fur coats for me and three for herself. Finally she bought a new car. After fixing her car for years it felt good not to get stuck on the road and have to call for help.

She was living in Bryan's basement at the time she won. There was a house across the street for sale for $72,000. She couldn't afford it and had to get a loan. We went to the Building & Loan and filled out an application. She was so worried about getting it. The President of the company was a friend of ours. She knew him when they were teenagers. Just before she won the loan was approved. The day we went to pick up the check, we walked in and said we won't need the loan. He did not see the news on TV and was surprised that she didn't want the loan. When she told him, he said: "Now you can buy the bank." She bought that little house and then she bought another one, a little bigger than that one. In case I had to live with her again one day, she had a bedroom in the little house, on the first floor, so I wouldn't have to climb the stairs to the other bedroom on the second floor. In the bigger house there is a three room private apartment, a separate wing of the house, in case Ben and I had to move in one day.

Bernadette founded Mary's Fund Foundation of which I am the President.

Jerry and Lynda are on the Board of Directors. Bernadette put $2 million into it.

One of Ben's daughters is in charge of a clinic. They are short on funds. The patients in the clinic are very poor and get free treatment and medicine. Otherwise they would have to suffer and maybe die without the clinic's help. She doesn't get much of a salary. There are hundreds of people that are being helped. What a good life to live. She believes in her work. There are a lot of good people in the world. Thank God for them.

I was thinking of starting a care home, taking care of eight people. So many of my friends needed one. Before I could do it, fate took a hand and I needed to be taken care of. I had a heart attack almost three years ago. If you don't pay attention to the signs of a heart attack, it might be too late. Three nights in a row I woke up because my arm fell asleep. I got up and walked a while and it was better. The third day I was cleaning the bathroom and couldn't finish. I was so tired I let it go until later. Ben and I went out to lunch. I couldn't eat much and was tired walking to the car. We got home and I couldn't stand up. We had a sofa near the door and I sat down, almost fell down. Ben was talking to me and I couldn't answer him. He didn't know I was so sick. Neither did I. He said he was going to go and water the pigeons. Before he came back I got enough strength to go to the kitchen and get an aspirin. I took it and called Bernadette. She was not too far and came right to the house. Her friend worked in the hospital and she called her to ask what her opinion of hospitals are. She told her St. Joseph was her choice.

Just then Ben came in and found out it was serious. He is not good taking care of sick people. She took me in the car to St. Joseph hospital. I thought I would be home that night. After the Doctors took some tests, they said I could go home but if I did I might not make it back in time. I stayed and had a triple by-pass. Jerry had one 20 years ago and he suffered much more than I did. When he told me how painful it was going to be when they took the tube from my neck, I was scared and waited. It didn't hurt at all. What they can do in twenty years with research. I had the best Doctor. He was teaching all the other doctors how to operate on people with heart attacks. A day before my operation was Easter Sunday. Bryan and his wife took care of taking the basket to church to get it blessed. They brought it to the hospital and the nurses let the whole family into the room at one time so we could celebrate Easter.

We all took a piece of bread, sausage and egg and wished each other a happy Easter. I don't remember but I didn't eat the food. Just a crumb maybe. I had a roommate and she complained it was too much noise with everyone there at once. Only a few stayed and the others went to the waiting room. The nurses wouldn't say anything because they loved Bernadette. They called her their angel. When someone wanted something, and the nurses were busy, she helped the patients. They didn't make her leave after visiting hours were over. They even brought her an extra pillow so she could sleep on the lazy boy chair. She stayed one night and Jerry spent one night.

After the operation Bernie ordered a private room. It had a love seat in the room that she slept on. When I was released from the hospital, she took me to her house. She was still working but Jerry came to stay with me until she came from work. Lynda stayed a few days. I had a lot of care. Jerry cooked some of the meals for me. When Lynda stayed she cooked. Everyone was there to help when I needed someone. When I had visitors they prayed with me. I couldn't read my prayer book for about a month. I didn't miss one day. Mary Kate read the whole book when she came to visit. That is Jerry's daughter. David his son cooked a pot of shrimp stew and brought it to the house. It is good to have a big family.

We have a big bedroom. We had two beds, adjustable ones. I couldn't sleep on the bed for about two months. I was more comfortable sleeping in the lazy boy chair. There were three in the room and a love seat. Ben came to visit but wasn't ready to move in yet. He had to get his pigeons sold. Instead of getting less, he kept on getting more to take care of. I knew he wouldn't be happy without his pigeons so I didn't nag him about getting rid of them.

After about a year, Bernadette quit her job. I was feeling better and we started to go to the casinos to play the slots. I made a few bus trips and decided to retire. It would be 50 years since I started. I wanted to treat the people who went on the bus with me, so I made six trips free for them. I won't quit going. I won't be running the bus trips any more.

I found something else to do. I went with Jerry to his agency and signed up for making commercials. About a week later I got my first job. It paid $150 an hour. I only had to sit on a bench and they took my picture. It was in the AARP book that gets printed once a year. It is given to all the Senators, Vice President, President, etc. I hope they call me again. You are never too old to work. Ben is 88 and still working every day. He does have two helpers now.

We celebrated Christmas eve at Bernadette's house. Ben and the family had time to come to the house. There were 23 in the family. We had two folding tables in the living room and the dining room seated eight. We didn't have to take turns. It was almost like my mother's Wigilia. There was Ben, Bernie and I, Jerry and his two children and two grandchildren, one son-in-law and daughter-in-law, Lynda and Pat and their three children and five grandchildren.

Easter we celebrated in the same house, with the blessed food, which Bernadette and I took to the church to get blessed.

Mother's Day we went to the country club. Jerry is a member and he made the reservations. Bernadette bought me a condo in Ocean City.

Father's Day we also went to the country club. All 23 came to the dinner. I was so glad everyone spent some time with Ben. A month later he started complaining about being dizzy. He wouldn't go to the Doctor. We kept trying to take him for a checkup. He kept putting it off. In August we had to go to Ocean City to pick up some papers. We spent some time with Ben before we left. He called me that night and said he was busy getting 400 pigeons ready for a man to pick them up the next day. I said I would call him as soon as I got home. The next morning his helper called and told Bernadette he was gone. She wouldn't tell me until we got home. He died in his sleep and they found him in the morning. He didn't get a chance to move into the house. He put it off too long.

In my prayer book there was a prayer that said if anyone keeps this paper in their house, they will see the Blessed Mother forty days before they died. When we met Ben for lunch forty days before he died, he told me he saw the Blessed Mother. Every day after that he kept telling us to do this or that after he's gone. He even wrote a will a few days before. He told his worker it won't be long. We went through almost the same thing a year before so we didn't take it seriously. We should have. I'm glad he was so close to the Blessed Mother. He even built an altar in the front room after I went to be with Bernadette.

Our Blessed Mother might have been with him since I wasn't. I pray every day that she is taking care of him now. Ben left the property and pigeons to Bernadette and Jerry. Bernadette is not selling the pigeons until she has to. It feels like Ben is happy about that. Two of my grandsons say that they saw him one time. It didn't scare them, they felt at ease. One of the workers at the place saw him too. He was pointing at the pigeon coops and trying to tell him something. Imagination or ????

On some of our trips to Atlantic City we saw some shows and met some of the actors and singers in person after the show. We played Bingo in some of the casinos. There are other things to do besides playing the slots.

My next trip will be to the new casinos in Pennsylvania. They are for the people I am treating because I am retiring after 50 years. One is in Chester, PA and the other is in Wilkes Barre, PA. I heard that they are very beautiful casinos. Of course they will be, if we win.

The family is trying to start a business of some kind. Bryan is interested in something to do with computers. I have not worked with them, so I don't know that much about them. But it is what he wants to do so I hope he succeeds.

Zachary graduated from the video school and lighting. He wants to start his own business. I hope he finds a lot of jobs. He has three children and a wife to support.

Heather graduated as a mechanical engineer but now she doesn't like that job. She is tutoring her cousin who is in high school That is a nice job. It is good to do something you like.

Lynda helps Bernadette with all the papers and mail that come in. She has her hands full.

Jerry is thinking of the biggest job. He has been an actor since he was in college. He has been in about a hundred plays, some in dinner theatres. His dream is to have his own theatre. If anyone can do it, he can. He has been an actor, a director and a worker in dinner theatre. He has experience in all the jobs in the theatre. I hope to go see him in his own theatre soon.

Bernadette's favorite charity is anything that has to do with abortion. She attends the fund raisers and meetings whenever she can. She helps them financially too. One day she wants to have a movie studio or work with someone in the movie business.

Ben was busy talking care of the pigeons, so I was his secretary and answered the phone. Once I talked to a Rabbi from the Holy Land. The Rabbi came to America on business and he stopped at the house to see the pigeons. He said he only had an hour, but stayed a few hours and had to take a later flight home. He came into the house to meet me and gave Ben and me a Jewish blessing. It's a little longer than any others I received. He invited me to meet his wife if I ever took a trip to the Holy Land. His community is on the Mount Zion, where the Blessed Mother died when she was at the well—that's what I read once. He took four pigeons back with him. They only charged $54 for air fare. They were all well and healthy when he got home. They take good care of animals on the plane.

Most of my time is spent praying for the ones in our family that don't go to church. When Bernadette graduated from high school and decided not to be a nun, she didn't go to church either. It took me ten years to pray for her to go back to church. I must not be doing a good job now for the rest of the family. It's been over ten years. I will keep praying as long as I live. If they all come back I will change it to a prayer of thanksgiving.

Before Ben died he was helping me to plan a birthday party for Jerry. It was a surprise for his 60th birthday. We were deciding where it was supposed to be held. After he passed away, Bernadette helped with the party. We decided on the country club. Since Jerry was a member he might not suspect anything. Patricia, my niece, pretended it was for her family and she asked him if she could use his name. Her father had worked at Bethlehem Steel and she made it sound like it was sentimental to have it there. He believed her and was surprised when he walked in the door and everyone shouted: "surprise!" In the doorway was a cardboard statue of Peter Pan, which Bernadette had Zachary make up. It was about five feet tall and had a picture of Jerry's face on it. He always wanted to play Peter Pan in a play.

The family was there, about 72 of them. We also got in touch with his friends from the old neighborhood since they were in grade school. Almost all of them came. One lived in Florida and couldn't make it. Another was killed in the war, we think. We're not sure. We couldn't find out if it was true or not.

Bernadette made up a little skit and we played it out. She had a doll that I put up under my blouse. When I took it out, it had Jerry's name on it. That's when he was born. Then she had a fishing rod, the boys used to go fishing. One day the girls and I went with them. Jerry said not to bother them, so I rented a rowboat and we went to the other side in the boat. About a half hour later they were calling us to come and get them. They probably didn't have any luck where they were and wanted to try catching some fish in deeper waters. They didn't mind the girls being with them as long as it was to their advantage. Then she had someone come out with a couple of golf balls. He liked to play golf.

She had a box of dog biscuits to remind them of the time they were painting the bedroom and one of the boys got hungry and ate the whole box of dog biscuits. When Bernie looked in the box it was empty, none left for the dog. Boy, was she mad at them. Then came the baseball bat. When Jerry was five and Bernie was three years old, Jerry told her to hit him. She was supposed to pretend to hit him with the bat. But she hit him before he finished telling her it was supposed to be a game. She was too fast and hit him with the bat. He didn't play any pretend games with her any more. It's a good thing I was there when they were playing cowboys and Indians. She had a gun in her hand, a toy gun. The name of that skit was "This is Your life." He is retired now but still keeping busy with what he likes to do best—acting and directing. I am sure he will remember this party for a long time.

I remember one of my birthdays. It was a surprise too. I was 76 years old. Bernadette couldn't afford to do it when I was 75 so she put "75+" on the cake. Several priests came to my party. They sang a special song in Polish and Bernadette gave me the microphone and told me to sing also. Good thing I remembered the song, the priests stopped and I had to sing solo. Ben was still with us and he left the pigeons and took time to be at the party until it was over. A few neighbors and some people from my bus trips joined us. About 100 people were helping me to celebrate the most memorable birthday ever.

I had a surprise birthday party for Bernadette. She didn't suspect anything. She was 57 years old. One of the girls she went to school with keeps in touch with her. She contacted a few of their classmates and they were able to come to the party. One of the Bishops came who is retired but still works at one of the churches we go to for Mass when we are home and not traveling. We had over 100 people. We rented the hall next door to Ben's house. I will never surprise her again. She doesn't like to be surprised. She didn't mind surprising me.

When I had my mother's 75th birthday, she was getting senile and didn't remember everyone who came to the party. There were only about 75 family and friends who came. The family wasn't as large as it is now. The children grew up and got married and had families of their own.

MEMORY LANE

Remember when the gas was cheap but you couldn't get it? If you were on the even days and you ran out of gas, too bad. You had to wait for the odd days. Now you can get gas any day, but you might have to wait until the day you have enough money to pay for it. Of course, there are always credit cards. Lots of people spend so much using credit cards, they could buy a house, a fixer upper. That way you get it cheaper. It takes a lot of work but saves a lot of interest.

One day we ran out of gas on our wrong day. I must have sounded really desperate. The gas station attendant filled up the tank when all I asked him for was a few gallons to get us home, until we could get some the next day. Maybe he was thinking of the time that millionaire stopped at a gas station and the worker there was so helpful, he left him a lot of money.

On our trip cross country we were traveling in California on Route 1 and we started to drive up a mountain. It took all day and no restaurants were on that road. Good thing we had a bag of snacks. We had breakfast, lunch and dinner in that bag. Only three of us, Bernadette, Bryan and I were on that trip. It got dark and the road was getting narrow. It was scary driving at night. We were getting low on gas. Just then we saw a gas station. They were closed. We had no choice. It was time to rest anyway. We took a nap and were awakened by a knock on the window. The man from the gas station knew we ran out of gas. He opened up and filled the tank with gas. It took about an hour to get off the mountain and get to a restaurant. Any one would do then. Bryan didn't mind, he slept half the time. We had the van and in the back was a little mattress, so it was comfortable for him. It softened the bumps in the road.

When I went to the church one morning, it was closed early. I thought of going across the park to St. Elizabeth church. I didn't know if they had a later Mass but I took a chance. The children went to the altar. I thought they were going to kiss a relic. When I got close I saw a casket. A bishop had died and he was in the casket and I got to kiss his ring. I didn't know before that day that he had died.

Our church had never closed that early
before. A few years before, I wanted to
buy a statue of St. Joseph for St. Alphonsus
church in memory of my brother Walter.
They already had one and asked if I would
buy a chair the bishop uses when he comes
there for special occasions. I decided to
buy it and the Bishop came there a few
weeks later. The priest in charge there told
the Bishop I had just bought the chair. I
didn't meet the Bishop in person but was
there when he died. Coincidence?

I remember going to my aunt's house
in Locust Point. We took the ferry boat
at the foot of Broadway and went across
the water and had to walk about a half
mile up the hill to get there. My cousins
used to go to the train station and when
they brought some trucks in full of coal,
they waited until they emptied the train.
A lot of pieces of coal would fall on the

ground and they gathered them up in some buckets they brought with them and took them home to burn in their coal stove to heat the house with. I wish I could have taken some home. We could really use them. It would have been enough to heat the three rooms we had instead of just the kitchen.

When my youngest brother got married he put in an application to work for the IRS. He didn't wait for them to call him, he got a job in a brewery. It didn't pay as much but it paid the rent and the other necessities. It took about a year but he finally got the job. Imagine how much rent he would have owed if he waited and not taken a lesser job. Sometimes you have to start at the bottom of the ladder so you can climb up.

Bernadette told someone I walk around the island 25 times a day. They said you must be really rich to own an island that you can walk around. They pictured an island like in the Bahamas. She was talking about the island in the middle of our kitchen. It has a marble counter top with a range in the middle. On one side there are four chairs so you can sit and eat your meals. Cabinets on the bottom for pots and pans and on one side a wine cabinet. Holds about 20 bottles of wine. The other side has shelves for knick knacks or other items. I don't need any machines for exercise, that island is just right for me.

Last year we were in Atlantic City and went to St. Nicholas church. They have a gift shop and it was Bryan's birthday in about a week. I thought I might find a nice gift for him. Lynda and Pat were with us and they went into the shop too. Bernadette and Lynda went into one room and Pat and I went into another room. As soon as I walked in I saw a crucifix on the wall. It was about a foot long and the image of Jesus looked so real. It was as if he was alive. We walked closer to get a better look. The right hand of Jesus came down and waved as if to say: "This is it, Bryan's birthday present." My vision is getting worse and I thought I was seeing things. I turned to Pat and asked him if he saw what I saw. He said he saw the hand come down and wave. We just stood there for awhile and couldn't say anything. The priest came in and I asked him if it was for sale. He took it down and said it was. The price was $25. I said I'll take it. It was hand carved and there was only one there. Bernadette and Lynda came in and they wanted one. The priest looked all around and couldn't find any more. He said they didn't know how it got there so he couldn't order any for them. Pat said Bryan won't want it but I wrapped it up and gave it to him for his birthday. When he heard the story of how I bought it, he said he will take special care of it and never give it away. He was very happy to get it. Whoever carved it has a special talent. It is very beautiful and the wood is different than any other I've seen. I'm glad Pat was there to see it.

When Jerry was a year old I was still living with my mother. It was a little crowded and Ben thought of building a house. We bought a lot and he started to dig the foundation and he and his friends were going to build the house. Except the part they couldn't do. They would have to get someone to help, a licensed person. We did not have enough money for the materials so I went back to work. My mother took care of Jerry.

I didn't earn too much before I had to quit. Bernadette was to be born. There goes our dream house. We bought a house in the city, two doors away from my mother's house. Ben was a little disappointed because he liked to build things. We sold the lot and made a few hundred dollars more than what we paid for it. The house we bought was really a wreck, a fixer upper. He was good at that so it didn't take much to fix it up. He had it done two weeks after Bernadette was born. My sister had gotten married and needed a place to live, His brother was looking for an apartment. The house was perfect. It was a three apartment house. My sister took the third floor. We had the apartment on the first floor. With the rent from the two apartments, I didn't have to worry. The mortgage payments were paid with the rent.

We had a lot of fun for six years in that house. After two years his brother bought a house and moved out. My other sister got married and she moved into that apartment. After two years she had a baby boy. When he was a year old she had a baby girl who only lived five days. Two years later is when my brother died and we bought the store and everyone moved because they bought a house. My mother moved with my other brother and his wife. He was in the navy then.

REFLECTIONS OF LIFE EXPERIENCES

One Year my daughters and I went to Disney World. We went to se a show that starred John Davidson. We were a little late going in and the only seats we could find were in the first row, three of them. Just enough for the three of us. He came walking down to the stage from the back of the theatre. He kept singing and shook hands with some women on his way down. When he came to the first row and shook my hand, his grip was so strong he pulled me from my seat and pulled me toward the steps that lead to the stage. It was so unexpected, I did not know what to do. He started dancing and still kept on singing. I danced with him and when he finished singing he knelt down. I said: "what do I do now?" I sang the last line and he said: "that was great!" The audience thought so too. I got a lot of applause. It lasted long enough for someone to take a good picture. A couple in the front said they would send me a copy when they got home. About a week later I received it. They wouldn't accept any money for the picture or the stamps. You meet some nice people some times.

THANK YOU CARD

It is almost 50 years since I started working on the bus trips for our church. Some people have been going with us for over 20 of those years. I thought it would be nice to show them how much I appreciated having them with me all those years. I treated them to six free bus trips. On my last one, they gave me a thank you card signed by all on the bus. I will miss them. Some I'll see in church or on other bus trips.

REFLECTIONS

In 1971 I went to Europe. My first plane trip. I went with my mother. When we were in Warsaw, a priest in the group wanted to surprise us. He got a few dozen people together and took us for a walk. We kept on walking down the same street a few times. We thought he was lost. He was stalling for time. We got to the square where everyone goes shopping and in the middle of the square is a church. Every hour a man goes up in the tower of the church and plays a bugle from all four sides of the tower. When we got to the corner we started to hear the music and all of a sudden there was a huge roar of a motor. It drowned the sound of the music. A man across the street had trouble with his car and was trying to fix it. The priest kept shouting for him to stop but he didn't hear him. The noise did not stop until the man stopped playing. We didn't miss it altogether. The next day the group went to the square and we heard it again. It wasn't as nice as at night because the square was full of people. It wasn't as quiet as at night.

The next day we went to the square by ourselves. The hotel was within walking distance and three of us went together. There is a restaurant in the square where Pulaski used to go. Most tourists like to go there. We didn't eat there because we were having dinner at the hotel. We just had a drink and left. As we were walking back to the hotel, that drink took effect on us and we started singing. Their drinks are pretty powerful. People passing by us were laughing at us. We didn't care. We were having lots of fun. We were still a little woozy when we got to the hotel.

Every hotel we were in had a piano in the dining room. One of the priests would play it and the group would sing, if they knew the lyrics. A lot of them did know them. It felt like we were at a wedding every night. If you're lucky to go on a trip with a nice group, you can really enjoy yourself. My mother and I were lucky. A Doctor and her aunt were with us most of the time.

This is a story my mother told me. It was about 1895 and my grandmother went to work for a wealthy family in Poland near the Russian border. She worked as a maid. They had a son who was away at school. During the summer, he came home, they fell in love and they got married. They had two daughters, my mother Mary and her sister Jeanette. My grandfather was a cousin to the last czar, Nicholas II. When my mother was two years old, her father was going to the royal ball at the palace. His wife was not invited. Only relatives were invited not their wives. He was all dressed up in his uniform, he was a guard at the palace. My grandmother didn't like him going without her. He was sitting down and my mother was on his lap playing with the shiny buttons on his uniform. They were in separate rooms and my grandmother was shouting and arguing with him from the other room. When he stopped shouting she came in to see why. He had a heart attack and died. He was

32 years old. He left my mother and her sister a lot of money. They couldn't have it until they were 18 years of age. Also my grandmother was left enough to buy a large farm where her family lived in Poland.

She got married to my step grandfather, who was very mean to my mother and her sister. One day he was angry and hit my mother with a branch from a tree. My grandmother saw him and saved my mother from getting hurt. When my mother was about ten she was so sick they thought she was going to die. Her mother dressed her in a white dress and laid her in bed expecting the worst. A gypsy told her to plant a potato in the back yard. The next morning my mother got well.

Her sister was sent to America when she reached the age of sixteen. She got married and my mother joined her at fourteen. Her boat was the last one to leave Poland. The war had started.

Their boat hit an iceberg, but it didn't sink. They made it to New York. When she got off the boat, it was the first time she saw a black person. Her first thought was that people in America worked so hard they didn't have time to take a bath.

Her sister was married to a good man. He worked hard and took very good care of his family. My mother lived with them until they had two children. It got a little crowded in their apartment. She went to live with a family friend. There was a girl just her age and they became as close as sisters. They went to New York to work in the tailor shop. My father met her before they left. He went to New York and proposed to her. They didn't like living in New York and came back to Baltimore. When she reached 21 years of age she married my father. That was the start of a hard life for her. My father worked as a stevedore. He made a good salary but it went to the bars. He was an alcoholic. He didn't take the role of a father as he should have. They had six children and the 7th one died at birth. My mother went to work in a packing house as many women did. We lived in three rooms, two bedrooms and a kitchen. By the time I was born we had it a little better. When my mother first moved into the house, she had to carry water about two blocks until they had water put into the house. There was no bathroom, just an out-house in the yard.

Christmas eve was the most important day of the year. There is a Polish tradition and my mother kept it up every year. The family would get together. The children were sent outside to look for the first star in the sky. That was the one the shepherds and the three kings followed to find the stable where Jesus was born. I think they wanted to get us out of the kitchen while they cooked. The meal was all seafood, no meat. When we saw the first star, we ran into the house shouting: "the first star is out." We broke the blessed wafer we got from church and wished each other a merry Christmas and good health. After the meal we exchanged gifts. There wasn't any money to buy gifts, so we made whatever we could. If we found an old newspaper, we could make a fireman's hat, an airplane and we could draw a picture on a bag that was too torn to use. With a piece of wax paper on a comb you could have a harmonica. An old piece of string was used to crochet. Use your imagination. The most important thing was to do good deeds and offer them to Jesus. It was His birthday, not ours.

My brother Walter was really into gifts. When he was ten years old he worked in a bakery, next door to us. They didn't pay much, mostly a stale loaf of bread and buns were paid. He worked as an usher in the movies also. He saved a few pennies and for Mother's day he bought my mother a flower. He put a big sno-ball in a pot. He got it late at night, at the market and put it in our alley so my mother wouldn't see it. My father came home from the bar and kicked it and the pot broke. That hurt my brother. My mother still liked it as much as if it wasn't broke.

My eldest sister Ida had it hard. She took care of the four of us while my mother worked. She would sit in a rocker with my two other brothers on her lap. My sister Betty sat on one arm of the rocker and I sat on the other arm. Ida would sing Polish Christmas carols to us. We would sit for hours listening to her. When she was 12 she went to work in a pickle factory. The inspectors from the state came to see if any children were working there. Before he came in the children were told to stay in the bathroom until he left. It worked.

We couldn't afford to go anywhere on vacation in the summer. My mother took us to a farm to pick beans. They gave us a bedroom and a kitchen to use rent free. That way we got a vacation and we didn't work too hard. When we got tired, my mother told us to go sit under a tree in the shade but we were to look for the boss. When he came around we had to go and start picking beans again. The other mothers made their children work hard.

My sister Betty worked in the bakery next door until she could get a better job. I was about eight when I was baby sitting. We got paid with bread and buns. That was a lot more than any other people had at that time. We felt very fortunate to have so much. It was the depression and some people were starving.

Our rent was $8.00 a month. My mother didn't have enough to pay it. She sent me to pay part of it, the landlady liked me. I was still scared telling her. She didn't give me a sermon, instead I got a lollypop. I didn't mind going after that.

My aunt was having trouble with her husband and she came to stay with us. She asked my mother to move to her house when they got a divorce. We did. It was two miles away from school. There was a school a half block away but we didn't want to change schools, so we walked. It was only for two years. My aunt sold the house and we had to move again. My mother found a house for $900. She needed $100 for the down payment. No one would lend it to her and she was crying and my brother asked her why. She told him. He went to the other room and came back with a jar full of change. He counted $100 and gave it to her. That was the first house we owned. My brother was the best. He dreamed of having his own business one day. We lived in that house for seven years. There was a store for sale for $7,500. My mother sold the house and bought it for my brother. It was his money that made it possible to buy the house in the first place. I was nineteen and had a baby. I left my husband but he wanted to get back with me. I lived with my mother for a year before I went back with him. He did support me and the baby. My brother opened a confectionary store. It was a very good business. He didn't enjoy it long. After five years, he got a bad spleen and suffered for one and a half years.

My sister Ida got married and lived in the house. The store was in the same building. It got a little crowded and my mother saw a house two doors away from the store and told me to look at it. It was a three apartment house. It was a real rat trap. My husband was a handy man and could fix it up. We needed $200 for the down payment. He sold his old car for that $200 and we bought it. My sister Ida moved in on the 2nd floor. We took the first floor. My husband's brother took the 3rd floor. They had a seven year old daughter. We had a boy and a girl then. They got along very well. After three years they bought a house and moved. My sister Betty got married and took the 3rd floor. We had a lot of fun. We played cards until late at night. My sisters only had to go upstairs.

My brother Walter got sick and he couldn't work in the store. We all helped my mother to keep it open for him. He suffered for one and a half years and passed away at 33 years old. My mother wanted to move with my brother Tony. He was in the navy and had a wife and two children. So she lived with them until he came home. No one wanted to buy the store. I knew how to work it, so I bought it. We weren't getting along too well. I thought it would be good for me, I wouldn't have to go and leave the children with anyone. We were divorced after ten years of marriage. I thought I would stay in the store for five years and that turned into 35 years. It wasn't a hardship. The children went to a Catholic High School. Bernadette went to be a nun. She left after graduating high school.

My mother came back to live with us. My brother bought another house after the Navy and she didn't like living alone.

She helped by cooking for us. I wasn't a good enough cook. Jerry went to Loyola College. Lynda quit high school in her junior year. She got married for a few short weeks. Got a divorce and two years later married a nice guy. They are still married today. Jerry got married at 21 and got divorced about 20 years later. He was manager of a trucking company and later got a state job. He is retired now but is busy as an actor and a producer. He has two children and two grandchildren. Lynda has three children and five grandchildren, Bernadette is still single and I am living with her now.

In 1960 my mother had a stroke and was bed-ridden for six months. She got well and went to Poland for a month. In 1971 she visited her family in Poland again. This time I joined her. My first trip abroad. I met my cousins and aunt for the first time. Next year my mother had another stroke. It left her senile and bedridden for four years. It was easy to care for her. She loved to travel. Bernie bought a van so we could put her wheel chair in it. We closed the store for two months in the summer and went to Ocean City, Virginia Beach, Disney World in Florida etc. When we came home, she wanted to keep going. She loved it. So did we. Everyone helped take care of my mother. Especially Bryan, my daughter Lynda's oldest boy. He was with us so much, he lived with us. We were only a half block from Lynda. My mother died in 1976 at 78 years of age. My sister Betty died in 1978, two years after.

THE END

(according to MOM)

I 'll never forget going into the gift shop in St. Nicholas Church in Atlantic City, looking for a birthday present for my grandson. As soon as I walked into one room, I looked up on the wall and there was a crucifix. My son-in-law was with me and we both stood there looking at it. We both saw the right hand of Jesus come down and point to the cross and in my mind I thought he was saying: "this is the birthday present you are looking for." His finger pointed to it. I'll never forget the way His hand looked. I turned to my son-in-law and asked him if he saw what I saw. He said he did. At first I thought my eyes were playing tricks on me.

The pastor of the church came in the gift shop and I asked him if it was for sale. He said yes. He took it off the wall and I bought it. My daughter came in and looked at it and wanted one also. So did my son-in-law. The pastor looked all over and could not find another one. They asked him if he could order one for them. He looked at the order list and could not find where it came from or who brought it in. It was hand carved and looked like someone used a special wood. No one knew anything about the crucifix. So it was one of a kind.

They said my grandson would not like it as a gift but when I gave it to him on his birthday he loved it. He said he would treasure it always.

PICTURES

1943 A picture of me as a teen with my sister in riding outfits. We were going to go to take lessons to ride horses. We only went once. I was afraid to ride them. The horse was so big. It felt like I was on an elephant.

2001 I made a bus trip from our church one year on my birthday. Ben and his cousin went with me. We were in front of the Resorts and a girl was giving away coupons. I took one but they didn't. It was for a tournament inside the casino. 950 people took the coupons and played. Only ten people were chosen. I was one of the ten. We played again and I got the highest score. I won $1,000.

2003 Mom's cake from her 76th birthday party.

2004 Dad, Mom, Lynda, Bernie and Jerry.

1953 My mother, Ben and I, and
our three darling children. Our
little angels.

1967 Bernie High School
graduation with Dad.

I took a trip to Fatima, Portugal. Lucia is one of the three children who saw the Blessed Mother. I was standing in the doorway of her house. The two graves in the basilica are the two younger cousins, Jacinta and Francesco. The little chapel was built on the spot where the children saw the Blessed Mother. There are a pile of branches in front of it. The people took the branches of the little tree she stood on.

1985 me with Polish Cardinal
Glemp in Rome.

2005 Make a Wish trip to Disney.
Here I am with Bernadette and
Lynda in front of Cinderella's
castle with my princess crown.

2004 Ben's pigeon world. He had about a dozen pigeon coupes on about three acres of ground, right on the water. He was close to ninety years old and still working all day. He was a good role model for the younger generation to keep busy and stay out of trouble.

1948 Clockwise from bottom right: Ben, Jerry, my sister Ida and her husband, Ben's sister Wanda, my brother Walter, me and Ben's mother. The baby in my arms is Bernadette.

2002 Ben and I. The background
was put in later.

2003 Jerry got us on the Jay Leno
show. Me, Bernadette and Lynda
but Jerry couldn't get away to go.

2003 we got to meet MD Governor
Ehrlich. Ben, Bernadette and me
with the Guv in the back.

1992 me dancing with John Davidson.

2004 we met Cal Ripkin.

2005 the family having lunch with
Cardinal Keeler.

2006 Bernadette arranged for us to meet Clint Black, the country western singer.

2007 Jerry took Bernadette and I to meet Henry Winkler (the FONZ) at a charity event.

2005 my first commercial. Posing at a WDC transit stop for the AARP photo shoot.

2006 I am sitting in the Oriole's
dugout at Camden Yards at an
Oriole's fantasy day.

2006 Bernie and I. My hat was the hit of the event we attended, a funky formal. Everyone came up to me for a close up photo.

1990 my daughters and I making a
Star Trek tape in Disney World.

1989 My sister gave me a
necklace. She wanted to see how
it looked.

1943 at 16, that's me after I got
caught in the rain.

1971 Lynda and Pat's wedding.
Her gown was so beautiful and
so was she. What a handsome
couple.

1992 when Ben and I remarried (35 years after our first marriage and 22 years after Lynda's marriage), I wore Lynda's wedding gown. It just fit without any alterations. She said if a daughter can wear her mother's gown, why can't a mother wear her daughter's? So I did!

1949 Ben and I at my sister's
wedding.

1951 the three children

1953 three children again

1952 Bernie and I

1955 Christmas with Santa. Clockwise from left: Jerry, Bernadette and Lynda.

Ben passed away in August of 2006. The Senator Theater was kind enough to honor him in a memorable way.